Also by Chet'la Sebree

MISTRESS

FIELD STUDY

BLUE OPENING

TURN (W)HERE

TURN (W)HERE

a geography of home

CHET'LA SEBREE

THE DIAL PRESS
NEW YORK

This is a work of nonfiction. Some names and identifying details have been changed.

The Dial Press
An imprint of Random House
A division of Penguin Random House LLC
1745 Broadway, New York, NY 10019
randomhousebooks.com
penguinrandomhouse.com

Copyright © 2026 by Chet'la Sebree

Penguin Random House values and supports copyright. Copyright fuels creativity, encourages diverse voices, promotes free speech, and creates a vibrant culture. Thank you for buying an authorized edition of this book and for complying with copyright laws by not reproducing, scanning, or distributing any part of it in any form without permission. You are supporting writers and allowing Penguin Random House to continue to publish books for every reader. Please note that no part of this book may be used or reproduced in any manner for the purpose of training artificial intelligence technologies or systems.

THE DIAL PRESS is a registered trademark and the colophon is a trademark of Penguin Random House LLC.

Hardcover ISBN 978-0-593-59584-8
Ebook ISBN 978-0-593-59586-2

Printed in the United States of America

1st Printing

First Edition

BOOK TEAM: Production editor: Andy Lefkowitz • Managing editor: Rebecca Berlant • Production manager: Chanler Harris • Copy editor: Scott Heim • Proofreaders: Wes Alspach, Dan Goff, Brianna Lopez, and Lori Newhouse

Book design by Jo Anne Metsch

The authorized representative in the EU for product safety and compliance is Penguin Random House Ireland, Morrison Chambers, 32 Nassau Street, Dublin D02 YH68, Ireland. https://eu-contact.penguin.ie

for my family

I am an aggrieved daughter of a country that doesn't love me the way I love her.

—DOLEN PERKINS-VALDEZ

I did not tell you that it would be okay, because I have never believed it would be okay. What I told you is what your grandparents tried to tell me: that this is your country, that this is your world, that this is your body, and you must find some way to live within the all of it.

—TA-NEHISI COATES

Contents

Prologue

Turn Where?

POINT OF ORIGIN: Variable
DESTINATION: Unknown

(1) Buckle up; check your mirrors.

Travel has always sung a song I've loved, especially when its tongue is slick with the euphony of smooth transit. Rubber on road reminds me of the ocean—a hush of white noise I can count on to be both constant and variable. Concrete laps louder than asphalt, and the crash of rumble strips ensures I slow for tolls or wake fast from an accidental doze. The hum of it lulling my innards.

(2) Select a route.

You might ask yourself how I plan to start if I don't know where to go. But who among us is ever certain? Even with multifold road maps and GPS, detours and road closures force routes we wouldn't have chosen, ones we've never seen before.

(3) Pull off.

People travel for various reasons: experience, escape, education; pleasure, status, food; to seek aloneness, connection.

In it, I seek a groundedness.

(4) Read the reflective signs.

Travel can be good for us because otherness is good.

—EMILY THOMAS

(5) Merge.

Life is a blur of forest from train windows, all of it passing faster than I can process. No matter how quickly I turn my head, the trees vanish from my vision. But travel helps me move at life's speed—the relative motion making the pace of my brain and my existence more congruous. Spending time in new locales slows the world: a walk through a park touching tree bark, the stickiness of its sap between my fingers. I'm less likely to take time to touch grass when I'm at home, sorting through which bills are due. But out in the vast impermanence of an unfamiliar place, an unfamiliar experience, I am steadied by a fresh landscape inching into focus.

(6) Turn on cruise control.

But even when the world won't slow in transit, I can make room for disorientation, as I soar through postal codes like a time traveler. Because when I am somewhere new, I am *supposed* to be bewildered. I expect to wander, hand tight-fisted around directions, chin toward sky looking at street signs; that a shopkeeper in Quebec might hear the inflection of my "*bonjour*" and switch to English, ask if she can be of assistance. As someone who has rarely felt like I fit in—Black girl in a white school, poet among a family in finance and law enforcement, aspiring single mom surrounded by partnered-parent households—I am drawn to travel's acceptable otherness, to be somewhere I don't, and don't expect to, belong.

I will admit I am too romantic about this.

(7) Adjust speed.

When you're a tourist, people might treat you the way they would someone with Wisconsin plates driving the stop-and-start streets of downtown DC: with kid gloves or contempt—letting you cross three lanes to make a right turn or laying on their horn.

That's if you have the luxury of being a visitor they deem acceptable.

(8) Read the reflective signs.

> How you travel, never mind what for, depends on who you are,
> the resources you have access to, what you look like,
> and how the world perceives your very presence in it.
>
> —PADMA LAKSHMI

(9) Check your blind spot; change lanes.

Feeling like an outsider doesn't land the same when you're lost on roads you know, ones with which you should be familiar.

(10) Slow for incident.

In 1998, three white supremacists—Shawn Berry, Lawrence Brewer, and John King—offered a Black man, James Byrd, Jr., a ride home in Jasper, Texas. Byrd knew Berry, so he accepted the lift. Instead of taking Byrd home, the white men drove him to a remote location, where they beat him, chained him to their truck by his ankles, and dragged him for miles. Evidence suggests Byrd lived for half the time they pulled him down a rural, tree-lined road. He died from decapitation when his body hit the edge of a culvert.

(11) Be mindful of your intersections.

Five years later, in 2003, my mom told me of James Byrd, Jr., as I prepped for a school trip to Dallas. I, at fifteen, dismissed her concerns. Ten years after, fresh from grad school, I told her that I wanted to take a great American road trip; she suggested I go ahead and get a job instead. It would be ten more before she would tell me how she worried she'd never be able to protect me, her forever little girl—who was born four weeks early, in a body that has continued to be surly.

I was, and still am, her audacious, strong-willed little Taurus.

(12) Swerve around obstructions.

But there did come a time when my mother's anxieties became mine.

(13) Turn on your hazards.

After a drive from Pennsylvania to Vermont in summer 2016, carefully plotted with bathroom breaks in college towns, I arrived at an artist enclave. The small town bourgeoned with creatives attending a residency. We gave readings in the laundromat. Dominated the mic during the bar's karaoke night. Popped into the bookshop before returning to our studios to work. But even in this adult summer camp for creatives, the world found its way in with the ease of the wind in crevices.

During a reception, details of Philando Castile's murder crept into our phones, and a white painter asked me how I felt about racism in America, as if it were its dawn.

(14) Read the reflective signs.

> Considering new and unfamiliar things forces us
> to expand and rethink what we know
> . . . It forces us to question what we take to be obvious.
>
> —EMILY THOMAS

(15) Pull over.

Alone in my home for a full pandemic year, I asked myself: Why is travel's song such an earworm? What is it about its simultaneous time-lapse and slow-motion state that I keep continuing to replay? Why, despite its ability to produce anxiety, do I reject stasis, clamber toward movement?

As I pull my body through space, displace myself with intention, I can quell the disquiet about my place alongside people whose lives plotted a clearer trajectory: college, job, partner, house, child; maybe a dog in there somewhere. I have avoided orienting myself toward those destinations—mistrustful of the "safety" presented by those nuclear iterations.

But is my itinerancy its own trajectory?

Will my route, like this book, rove until novelty becomes familiar?

(16) Read the reflective signs.

> How do we decide where we belong?
>
> —TONI MORRISON

(17) Find your way back onto the road.

I've come closest to myself far from addresses I've listed on legal documents: under the full moon over Useless Bay; on a walk through the Chattahoochee woods; below the sun's glow on the Gateway Arch. In rented homes across America, I've learned to manage chronic pain; admitted to myself I wanted to be a mom, that I was queer; decided it was time to let go of people I've loved so I could, instead, love myself.

But where do I—single, Black, itinerant, aspiring parent—belong?

(18) Select next route. Start over.

Part One

WHERE ARE YOU FROM?

Root(les)s: A Genealogy

DISCLAIMER: *Some of these records have been redacted; the archive is incomplete.*

RECORD TYPE: Surname Tree
SUBJECT: Chet'la N. Sebree

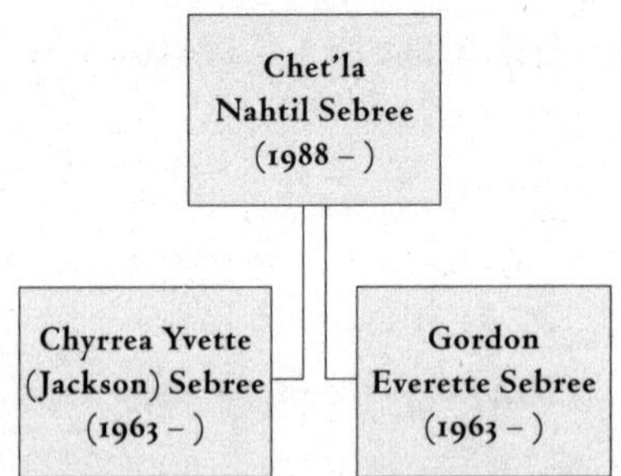

RECORD TYPE: Places of Residence
SUBJECT: Chet'la N. Sebree
LOCATIONS: Claymont, Delaware
New Castle, Delaware
Richmond, Virginia
New Castle, Delaware
Middletown, Delaware
Richmond, Virginia
Ravenna, Italy
Coventry, United Kingdom
Richmond, Virginia
Washington, District of Columbia
Lewisburg, Pennsylvania
Charlottesville, Virginia
Middletown, Delaware
Lewisburg, Pennsylvania
Washington, District of Columbia

DETAILS:

Chet'la N. Sebree was born May 15, 1988, to Chyrrea and Gordon Sebree. She is the second of their two children. She had an "all-American" two-parent, two-kid, one-dog household—different from the ones her parents were raised in. They took pride in this. Although she was born in Chester, Pennsylvania, she lived in Claymont, Delaware, for her first year before her parents purchased their first home in New Castle, where she would form her first memories—dancing in rubber boots at the top of the stairs, pumping her legs to reach new heights on her swing set. When she was five, the family relocated to Richmond, so her mother could attend law school, before they all returned to Delaware in 1997.

In 2001, her parents bought a house in Middletown, where their marriage unraveled over the next twenty years. Maybe it was always unraveling, but the move coincided with Chet'la's pubescent awareness and a new intensity of emotions. To make her parents' storied history short: they loved, but were not good for, each other. Her father's indiscretions were at the center of their dismantling. And her mother developed a propensity for not starting shit but making sure to finish it. The Middletown house would be the place Chet'la lived the longest.

When she turned eighteen, she began to perfect the art of leaving, occupying no residence for more than twenty-four months for the next eighteen years. An example of this: she studied abroad and lived in three cities the year she turned twenty. A therapist once explained to her that her tendency to leave might be linked to the place she left at eighteen, the place where, in one sense, she had the most stability, while also having the least of it. This may be why Chet'la claimed to reject ideas of marriage and family. She preferred the presumed safety of being a solo entity, the security of sometimes being lonely—even as she daydreamed of privately exchanged vows and child-rearing.

But even though she's always been willing to pack and go, she continued to come back to places that were familiar, wondered if they would be different when she returned.

RECORD TYPE: Travel Log
DATE: August 12, 2021
LOCATION: Middletown, Delaware
AUTHOR: Chet'la N. Sebree

TRANSCRIPTION:

To know me is to know my dad's my guy.

The guy I call when I need a guy, a fix-it person. I call him when my car battery is dead to ask if it's possible to electrocute myself with the jumper cables. I call him when I'm six time zones away, and I need to be coached through capturing a thousand-legger hovering over my bed. I call him when I'm a finalist for a prize I want to feel like I've already won or when I've struggled to get out of bed for three days and need him to remind me I'm not alone.

Some people think he's my guy because we look alike. Once, when we were walking through downtown DC, a passerby pivoted to say, "There's no denying her." At a JCPenney in my teens, while I was in Juniors and he was in Shoes, a man approached my father to tell him, "I don't know if you know, but someone over there belongs to you." And although we agree we look related, we don't think we "twin" the way my family and strangers have suggested. Still, sometimes when I compare photos of us at specific ages, I cannot refute the truth: my father and I not only share DNA, but a whole face.

But he's actually "my guy" because he's someone I like to hang with. He's the kind of parent to cut you some slack, to joke around. But sometimes he feels more like a sibling than a father, like a peer who takes on the role of an adult ^ or doesn't when the situation requires one. He kicks my ass at Uno and Clue, but refuses to play Scrabble, because he knows he'll lose. We laugh and drink margaritas while listening to Rihanna and the Chi-Lites—him snapping with his index finger and thumb as he shoulder-dances to the tune.

But as close as we are, there's so little I know about him; I am hoping this road trip we're taking through the Midwest, to his hometown, will change this.

RECORD TYPE: Surname Tree
SUBJECT: Chet'la N. Sebree

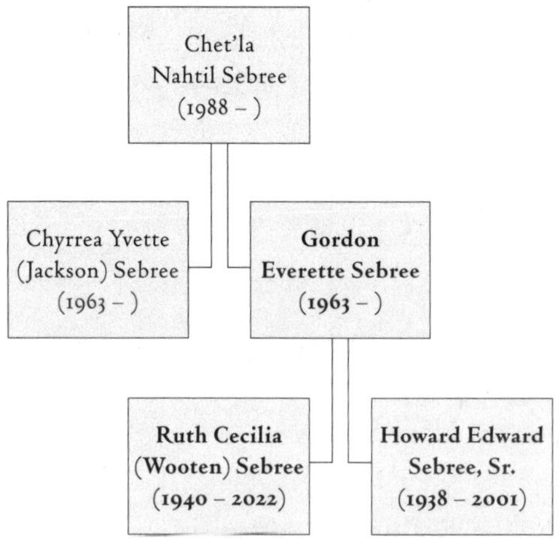

RECORD TYPE: Places of Residence
SUBJECT: Gordon E. Sebree
LOCATIONS: Indianapolis, Indiana
Orlando, Florida
San Diego, California
Naples, Italy
Staten Island, New York
USS *Estocin*
Chester, Pennsylvania
USS *Mount Whitney*
Claymont, Delaware
USS *Patterson*
New Castle, Delaware
Richmond, Virginia
New Castle, Delaware
Middletown, Delaware
Bear, Delaware
Middletown, Delaware

DETAILS:

Gordon E. Sebree was born July 13, 1963, in Indianapolis, Indiana, to Ruth and Howard Sebree. He is the fourth of their five children. The seven of them, which included three daughters and two sons, lived off and on together. For a year and a half, when his parents were separated and reconsidering their marriage, all the men lived in an apartment. Gordon's affinity for cleanliness, later thought to be a product of his twenty years in the military, developed during those apartment months, when he learned to care for himself.

On August 10, 1981, less than a month after he turned eighteen, he shipped off for basic training in Florida for the Navy. From there, he went to tech school in San Diego and then was stationed in Naples, Italy, for two years. During those early stints in the service, he saw much of the world's waterways, taking pride in peeing in every ocean (except he hadn't yet made it to the Indian).

In November 1984, his best friend, Tyler, whom he was stationed with in Italy, invited Gordon to his family's Thanksgiving in Chester, Pennsylvania. There, Gordon met Chyrrea, Tyler's cousin. Five months later, they would begin a life together with her four-year-old son. While Gordon was stationed throughout the Mid-Atlantic, when he wasn't on ships, he would make his home wherever they were. Shortly before having their second child in the late '80s, they moved to Delaware, where he's resided for over thirty years. Gordon never lived in Indiana again.

RECORD TYPE: Photograph
DATE: August 16, 2021
LOCATION: Arlington Middle School (formerly Arlington High School in Indianapolis, Indiana)
SUBJECT: Gordon E. Sebree

CAPTION:

My father stands, chest puffed, in front of his alma mater, building towering two stories above him. With his shoulders back, he splashes tall against his past—the man returned to his boyhood forty years later. But as soon as the shutter closes, I see him anew: his chin dips; his shoulders slump.

"I'm ready to go," he exhales.

RECORD TYPE: Travel Log
DATE: August 15, 2021
LOCATION: Indianapolis, Indiana
AUTHOR: Chet'la N. Sebree

TRANSCRIPTION:

For most of my life, my father has traveled to Indiana alone every year or so; the last trip we made as a whole family was when my grandfather died in 2001. As an adult, I've tried to come for big birthdays and reunions. Aunt J will tell me about her fourteen children, two of whom "went home to the Lord." DJ will reminisce about their high school shenanigans. Dad and I will go to the State Fair, where he'll eat elephant ears. A parade of chicken, green beans, and potatoes is often punctuated by a trip to Long's Bakery, from which he'll savor fresh glazed donuts, apple fritters, and bear claws. But this trip is different, as I pick at fibers to unspool the thread of him. We drove by the home where his mother's mother lived, down the street where he went drag racing; he showed me the bank his brother failed to rob, and the field where he was caught.

We spent extra time at his childhood home, which we'd previously only driven by. I snapped a picture of him under the DENNY STREET sign hung high on a pole, as he talked to the woman who bought the house from his parents forty years ago. He described how the seven of them survived in the small cube of brick—the girls' room and the boys'; his parents'. He animated how they played in the yard, and even took me down to the garage. Standing over the cracked concrete, he explained how each family member carved their initials in the poured cement: letters for Gloria, Ginger, and Gordon; Howard and

Buddy (Howard Jr.); and Rhonda and Ruth. Only one "H" remained.

There is a glee and gloom that rises and falls throughout each tract of this trip—the way I imagine the steering wheel sat precariously in his hands as he tore down streets like speedways. But I let my grip slip on our fast-driving car, felt the tires tip off their axis, when we went to see my grandmother and combed through photos of people painted faintly on my imagination. With a giggle as gripping as the gospels she loved, my Grandmom Sebree regaled us: stories about how she liked to dance as a girl and visiting her husband's Kentucky family land. She laughed her big laugh—the one both she and my father share, where their cheeks meet the crease of their under eyelids. This is why he still calls Indiana "home." His mother is here, and he loves her.

But the undertone of his sadness is inescapable. While he delights in showing me his world, he doesn't want to reveal that it was also full of hurt. He hides behind smiles while he points to his old haunts—the court where he used to play hoops; the shop where he served Lindner's ice cream scoops. These were versions of himself that he'd ultimately run away from. "I wasn't athletic"; "I wasn't popular"; "I had my group of friends, so I was okay," he would say, softening the sting of his memories. But here with him, I feel it, too; there just isn't enough good to cling to.

The weight of that sat heavy on my chest when he said, "When my mom is gone, I don't know if I'll ever come back here."

RECORD TYPE: Photograph
DATE: January 2020
LOCATION: Indianapolis, Indiana
SUBJECTS: Gordon E. Sebree & Ruth C. Sebree

CAPTION:

My dad dances with his mom, a foot shorter than him in her kitten heels, on her eightieth birthday. They sway—one of his hands on her back and the other holding hers. He would have her nuzzled against his chest if he wasn't bent at the waist, mouth agape, eyes squinted in a laugh that cracks open his whole face. Moments earlier, he leaned over to whisper, "I know I'm your favorite." To which she said, "Don't tell nobody."

Although in the image her face is obscured, the lift in her cheeks reveals she is smiling, as well.

We don't know this will be one of their last pictures together.

RECORD TYPE: Journal Entry Excerpt
DATE: December 2020
LOCATION: Lewisburg, Pennsylvania
AUTHOR: Chet'la N. Sebree

TRANSCRIPTION:

Nothing quite like having your therapist gently drag you within an inch of your life after your lymph node biopsy results come back negative for malignancy. She waited two whole sessions to bring up that she was surprised by what had you preoccupied.

It wasn't your deadlines or your job, your worry that your issues with your parents would never be resolved, or how they manifested in your resistance to partnership. It wasn't about what, if it wasn't cancer, the swollen nodes might mean. No. It was that you were worried you wouldn't get to have a kid; something, to her, in your year together, you'd never said you wanted.

This reminds you of when doctors discovered a mass on your right ovary three years prior—how, sobbing, curled on your bathroom floor, you asked your mom what if you never get to be a mother. She—worried in the moment you might have cancer, which you, again, did not—reminded you of your fear-filled confession, months later.

Which is to say, Chet'la, this isn't a new revelation. Just one you've been evading.

RECORD TYPE: Surname Tree
SUBJECT: Baby Sebree

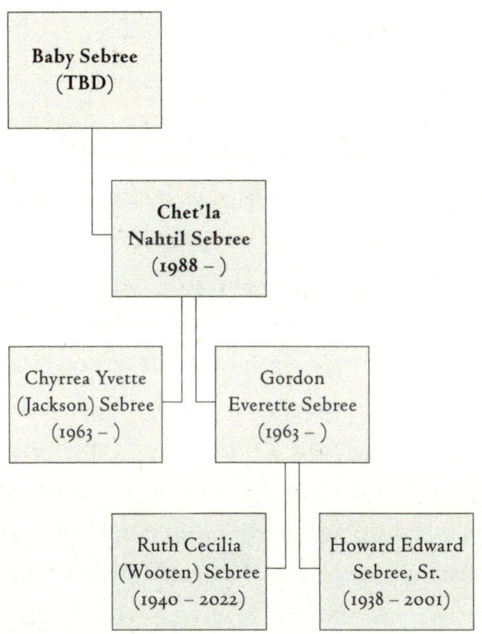

RECORD TYPE: Journal Entry Excerpt
DATE: June 2021
LOCATION: Lewisburg, Pennsylvania
AUTHOR: Chet'la N. Sebree

TRANSCRIPTION:

I'm so fucking relieved that Dad took it well. I mean, he was considerably more shocked than when I told him I wasn't *only* attracted to men, confirming his suspicions. But despite his initial question about how I was going to raise a kid alone (probably worried my plan is to climb back into his wallet, which, honestly, maybe it is?), he was immediately supportive. Maybe even a little excited? Maybe that's wishful thinking? I don't know.

He's such a good dad to me and my brother, already a good grandfather. He's always liked being a family man, even when there were parts of that role I wouldn't have given him high marks in. When my parents' marriage merged into what I saw as mostly façade—a production put on for cookouts—there was a part of him that still relished the role of husband and father. After they split, my mom said she thinks he was trying to be a better dad than the one he had.

RECORD TYPE: Photograph
DATE: 1968
LOCATION: Indianapolis, Indiana
SUBJECT: Gordon E. Sebree

CAPTION:

My dad is five in this wallet-sized photo, so says my Grandmom Sebree's handwriting. In a stark white shirt with a bow tie tilted to the side, under a dark sport coat, my dad smiles a full-cheeked smile. Even then, he didn't show all his teeth when he grinned. He's adorable, and I see my baby face in his. I want to reach through waxy film and time to hold him the way he so often held me—drying a tear and providing a warm, affirming offering.

He is around this age when his near-silent father, Howard, tells him that he looks like a monkey when he cries. My father is a child, so he doesn't understand that white people likening Black people to primates has its roots in colonialism and white supremacy. But what he does understand is that looking simian isn't a good thing, that his feelings make him less human. I imagine him, lower lip trembling, wiping off his face, and starting a life of emotional restraint that day. My heart hurts for the boy who learned not to embrace his soft, tender parts, for the kid who was worthy of a gentleness his father couldn't offer.

It is also around this age when he starts to play with his paper men. These are strips of paper he uses as toys, since his older brother broke his action figures. Belly flat to the floor behind his bedroom door, he pretends one of those rectangles is Batman—a man who has no special powers but wants to protect Gotham. Even though those strips are torn, they can still cut. And with them, my father goes to battle. His paper men, along with comics and westerns, are the portals through which he escapes to places better than the one in which he lives. In his imagined world, there aren't kids who taunt his weight or extension cords wielded like fists. In that imaginary space, I imagine there also are no tears.

RECORD TYPE: Research Note
DATE: August 2022
LOCATION: Lewisburg, Pennsylvania
SOURCE: *Rewriting Family Scripts: Improvisation and Systems Change* by John Byng-Hall

QUOTATION:

> "Family life is a rehearsal for the next generation. Each parent has scenarios from childhood which if repeated in this generation can be called 'replicative scripts.' Some childhood experiences will have been uncomfortable and attempts may be made by the parents to avoid these with their own children. This choice of opposite style of parenting can be called 'corrective scripts.' There are also parenting styles that are improvised, or are influenced by observing other families. . . . These can be called 'improvised scripts.' When comparing past and present, it is often possible to see elements of all three types of script in any scenario."

NOTE:

My father has been running corrective and improvised scripts in his parenting since I was young: choosing not to spank me; making sure I learned to roller-skate because he never did; creating space for my emotions.

I wonder which scripts my father also replicated.

RECORD TYPE: Surname Tree
SUBJECT: Baby Sebree

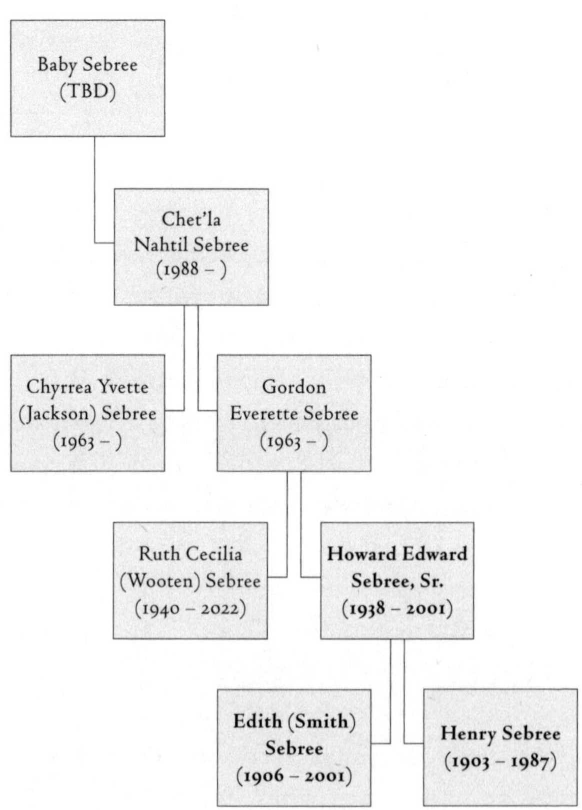

RECORD TYPE: Places of Residence
SUBJECT: Howard E. Sebree, Sr.
LOCATIONS: Trenton, Kentucky
Indianapolis, Indiana

DETAILS:

Howard E. Sebree was born October 26, 1937, in Trenton, Kentucky, to Edith and Henry Sebree. He was one of ten children. After moving to Indiana, he met and married Ruth Wooten, a mother with two daughters. Together, they also brought into the world two boys and another girl.

Howard was known for being quiet and stern; he died of diabetes-related kidney failure in 2001.

RECORD TYPE: Travel Log
DATE: August 17, 2021
LOCATION: Indianapolis, Indiana
AUTHOR: Chet'la N. Sebree

TRANSCRIPTION:

Why am I trying to find root in a place my father fled, in people who are already dead?

RECORD TYPE: Excerpt from Oral History
DATE: July 2020
LOCATION: Phone Call (Lewisburg, Pennsylvania, and Indianapolis, Indiana)
SUBJECTS: Chet'la N. Sebree & Ruth C. Sebree

TRANSCRIPTION:

CS: Do you know Pop-Pop Sebree's father's father's name?
RS: You mean Grandaddy Sebree?
CS: Who's that?
RS: Henry, Howard's dad.
CS: No, no, I mean Henry's dad.
RS: Sorry, honey, no. I don't.
CS: It's okay.
RS: But you know he was raised by white folks, right?
CS: What? I'm sorry, I mean—
RS: Yes. I believe he was adopted by white people, who raised him.
CS: So, wait, was Sebree his birth name or theirs?
RS: You know, I don't know.

RECORD TYPE: Surname Tree
SUBJECT: Baby Sebree

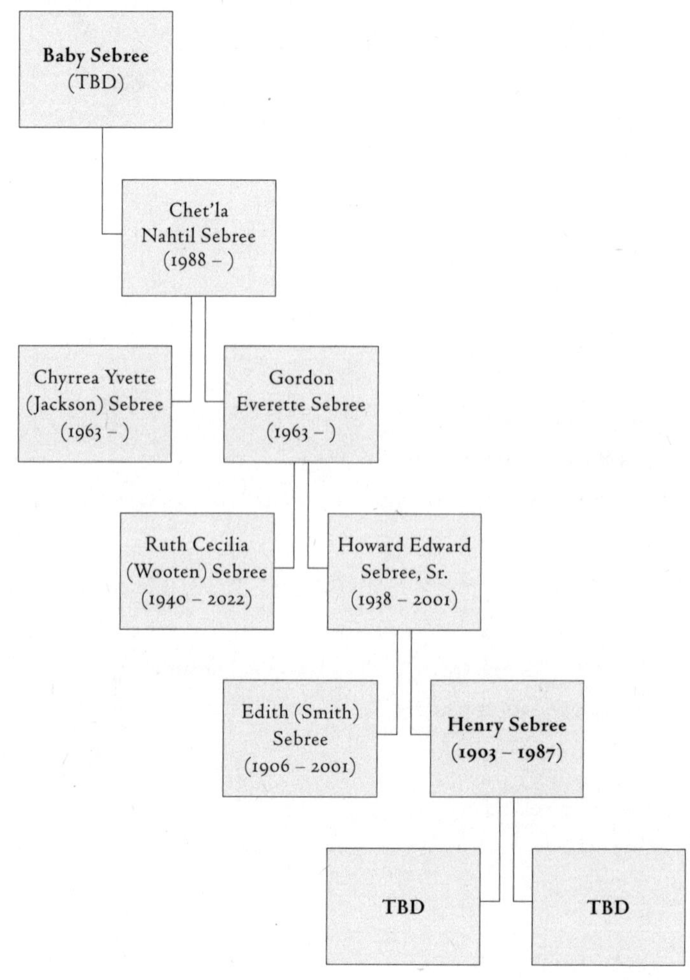

RECORD TYPE: Research Note
DATE: June 2021
LOCATION: Lewisburg, Pennsylvania
AUTHOR: Chet'la N. Sebree

TRANSCRIPTION:

So, this name I may pass on, to whom does it belong?

RECORD TYPE: Surname Tree
SUBJECT: Baby Sebree

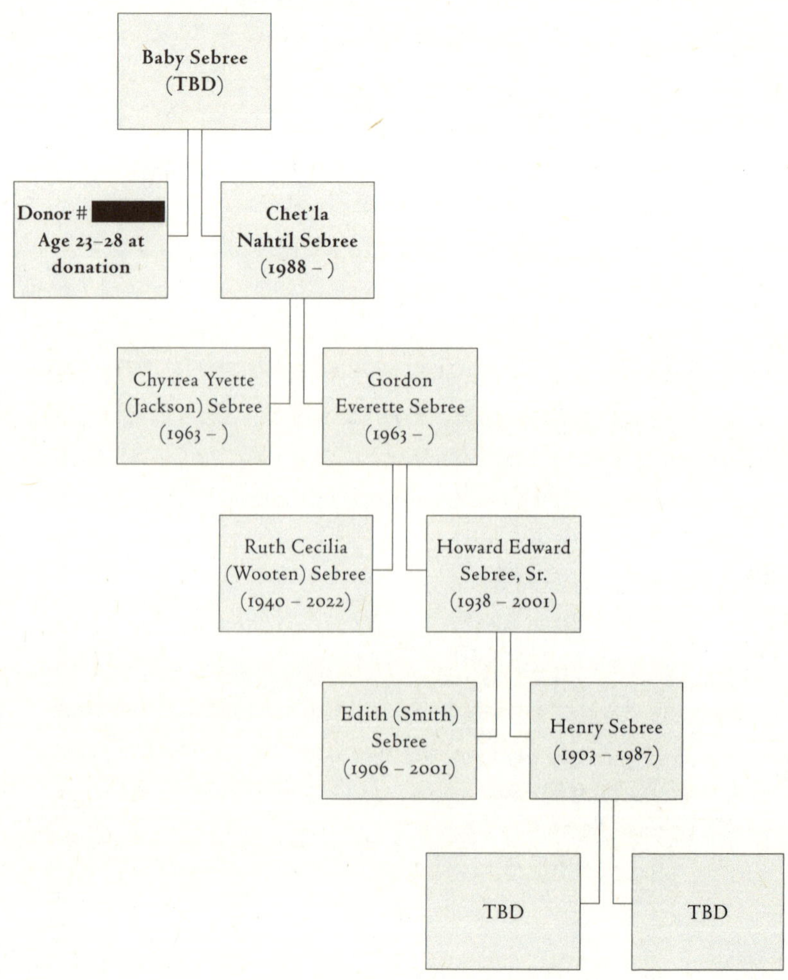

RECORD TYPE: Journal Entry Excerpt
DATE: May 2024
LOCATION: Washington, DC
AUTHOR: Chet'la N. Sebree

TRANSCRIPTION:

I keep putting off making my sperm donor decision, fearful I won't make the "right" call, as I scroll through profiles with heights and weights, star signs and age ranges.

I spent hours today looking at the same ones, making notes, hoping some magic voice would pop in and say *Here; this one.* I ticked off the suggested "nonnegotiables" according to Dr. █████: CMV status, genetic conditions for which I am a carrier. Then, I ticked the one thing I want: a Black donor. The combination of this narrowed the pool considerably: no donors at Seattle Sperm Bank, ten at California Cryo, four at Fairfax. Each clinic similar in its limited options.

From my lot, I read essays and listened to audio, sifted through their baby pictures, checked if they, too, have celiac or lupus. I sorted these strangers and their donations into maybe, yes, and no piles, with too many in the first category. *Maybe not* donor #█████, because of shared family history of diabetes, or donor # █████, because they are also a carrier for glycine encephalopathy? This is not *not* tricky. Some people can just roll over and make a baby without this complicated (maybe even a little problematic?) note-taking . . . That said, I really wish my friends would stop suggesting I just go out and fuck a stranger.

Will the "right" choice churn my gut like falling in love? Do I even remember what that feels like?

I want there to be a clear answer, though I know it still

wouldn't provide the resolution to other questions that clutter my waking hours:

> *Will I be a good parent?*
> *Will I be good at it but hate it?*
> *Will my kid hate me?*
> *Will I burn into them something so deep that it will never stop festering?*

RECORD TYPE: Journal Entry Excerpt
DATE: October 2023
LOCATION: Washington, DC
AUTHOR: Chet'la N. Sebree

TRANSCRIPTION:

In one of my core memories, my father sits on the edge of my parents' bed, crying. He does not look simian like his father suggested. He looks like some of the men who've gone on to disappoint me. I'm twelve, and my mother says, "Tell her." And with his response to those two words, I entered my parents' marriage, learned more details than any child ever should, and would continue to participate in their push-and-pull, even after the paperwork was processed on their divorce twenty years later.

My dad knows that bedside moment is a radioactive site for me, its contamination half-lifting ad infimum.

RECORD TYPE: Journal Entry Excerpt
DATE: July 2024
LOCATION: Washington, DC
AUTHOR: Chet'la N. Sebree

TRANSCRIPTION:

For eighteen years, my child may only know their other biological parent's donor number.

Maybe a single photo of them with a Santa.

Maybe siblings listed in a donor registry.

At eighteen, they may be able to contact this human, should that person still be alive and willing.

Until then, what can I tell them about those with whom we share a surname?

RECORD TYPE: Place of Residence
SUBJECT: Henry Sebree
LIST: Trenton, Kentucky

DETAILS:

Henry Sebree was born June 3, 1903 (I believe, after some digging), to William and Mary Lou Sebree in Trenton, Kentucky. He was born, raised, and stayed in the same place; he died in January 1987.

NOTE:

There were two Henry Sebrees listed as living around this time in Trenton, but my best guess is that the one born to William and Mary Lou is my relative.

RECORD TYPE: Surname Tree
SUBJECT: Baby Sebree

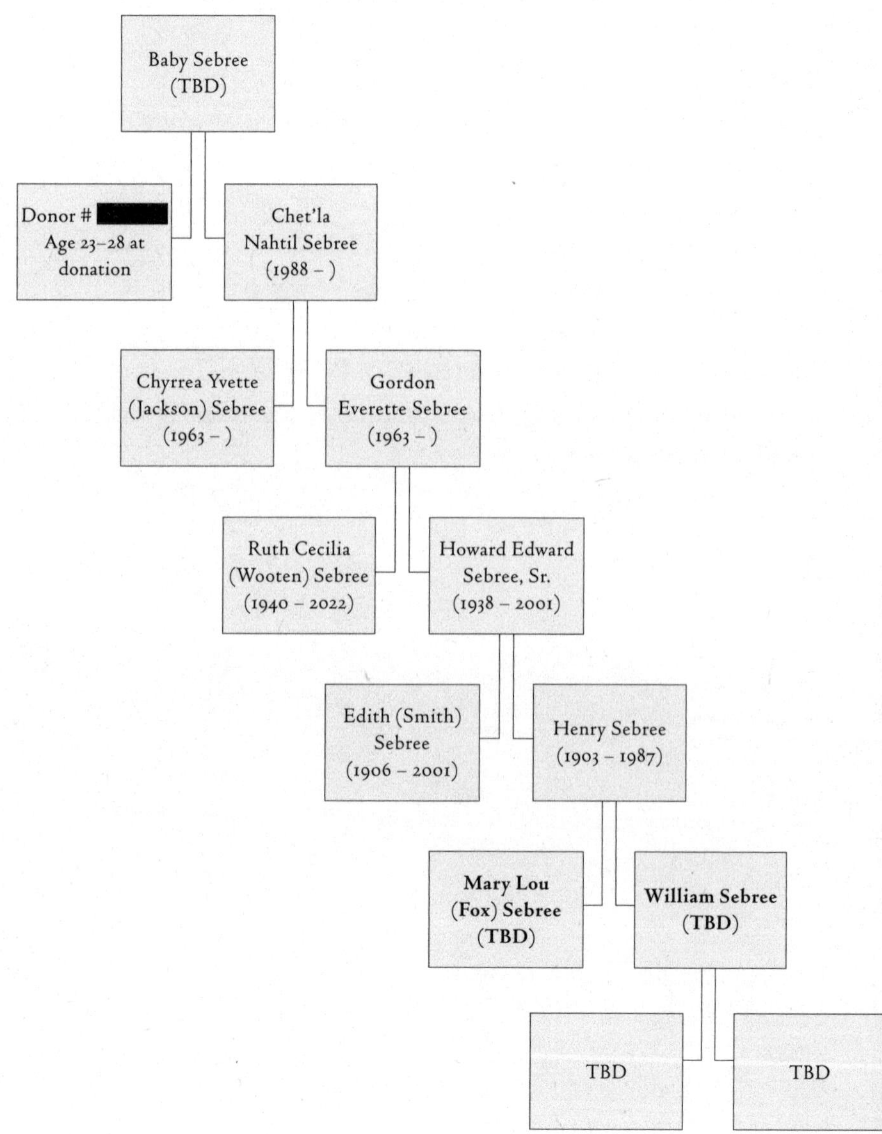

RECORD TYPE: Research Note
DATE: July 2024
LOCATION: Library of Congress (Washington, DC)
AUTHOR: Chet'la N. Sebree

TRANSCRIPTION:

I know little of the man who raised my father or the man who raised him.

What I definitively know: Henry raised Howard, who left Kentucky and settled in Indiana; Howard raised Gordon, who left Indiana and settled in Delaware. And Gordon raised me, who left Delaware and settled in DC.

Will my kid pick up and go? Run like my father and I ^and maybe Howard did from home?

Is rootlessness our inheritance?

RECORD TYPE: Journal Entry Excerpt
DATE: October 2024
LOCATION: Washington, DC
AUTHOR: Chet'la N. Sebree

TRANSCRIPTION:

I start bleeding several hours before the doctor tells me about the fertility treatment's failure. This is the third time I've received this call. This time I'm at my desk, gazing at the Washington Monument, when I feel the possibility slip against my cervix. In a public bathroom stall, I plead for the pink to be an implantation bleed, desperate for a child to take root in me.

RECORD TYPE: Surname Tree
SUBJECT: Baby Sebree

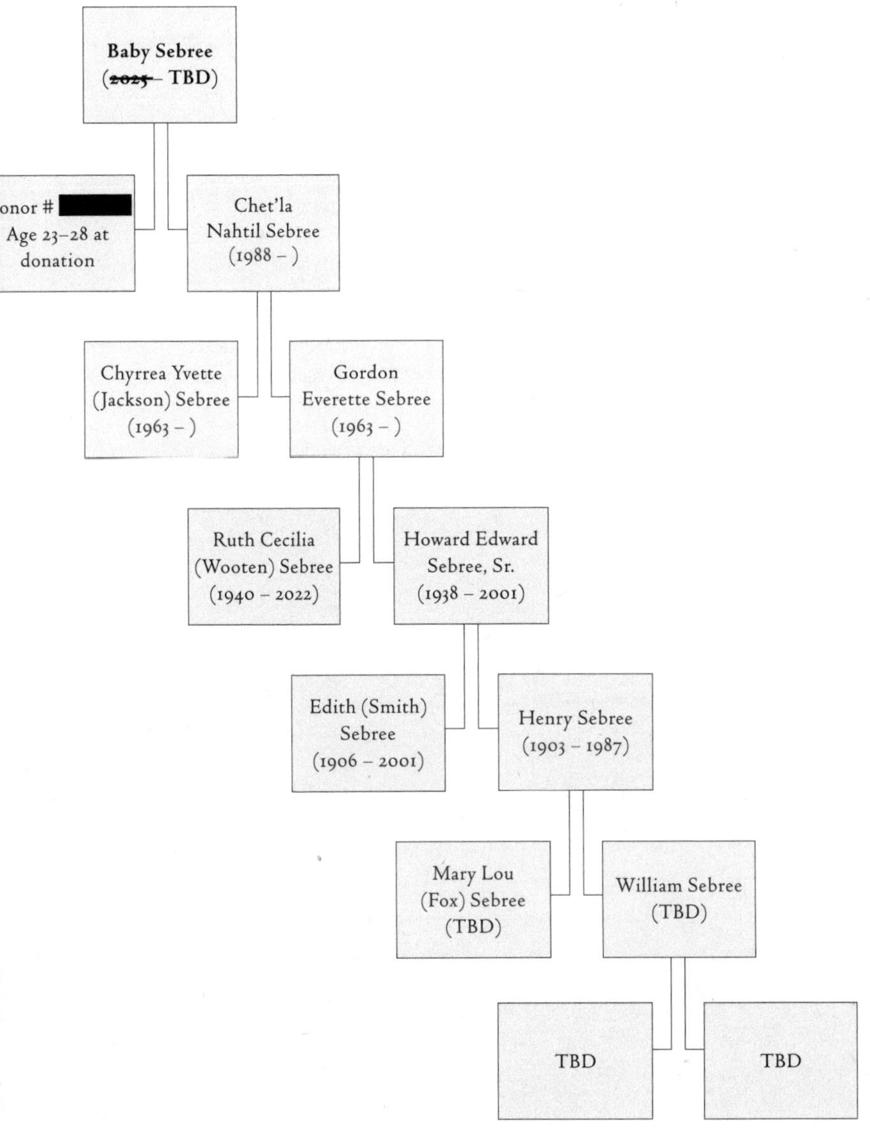

RECORD TYPE: Excerpt from Oral History
DATE: August 2021
LOCATION: White Castle (Lafayette, Indiana)
SUBJECTS: Chet'la N. Sebree & Gordon E. Sebree

TRANSCRIPT:

CS: I'm so worried that I'll fuck up a kid.
GS: Love them the way you wanted to be loved; that's what I did.

Partus Sequitur Ventrem

> Yet at the root of reparation is repair. My tooth will not grow back ever. The root, gone.
>
> —LAYLI LONG SOLDIER

Blood bonds matter to my mom; she sees them as unbreakable. Even when metaphorical anemia and lymphoma lurk within, she sees blood as the life source that it is. For her, family isn't the people you choose, but the people, by biology, you're yoked to. She's steadfast in this belief, which has its holes: my father isn't genetically related to my brother; my Nana, one of her favorite relatives, was my grandfather's adoptive mom. But those are exceptions to the rules by which she ascribes kinship.

I believe she became even more hematologically hemmed after she divorced my father when they were in their fifties. She laments that my brother and I don't live closer, wishing we could cozy up to her on the regular. In our absence, she nuzzles near other family members, even in their dysfunction—heralding them when it comes time to decide where to spend her holidays, declining invitations from decades-long friends. This has started to pivot a bit, but I wonder if her commitment to relatives is manifested from her desire to hold tight to the wisps of what's gone, hoping to remain tethered to those biological bonds. Maybe as a child of a divorce herself, she's held fast to ideas of family because she knows it could be fleeting like those crisp but warm early days of summer.

When she waxes poetic about lineage, she extols women who came before her. There's vivid longing in her descriptions of growing up in Chester, Pennsylvania, around her mother's people: the crackle of her Aunt Chris cooking chicken livers, the fuss of her mother ensuring her Sunday clothes were freshly pressed, the slop and sweat of her grandmother Ruth mopping to prepare for guests.

My mother fiercely loved Grandmom Ruth, a woman I remember being well into her late adulthood when I was a child. She was an elder who smoked cigarettes and cursed and asked me to come comb her hair. My mother remembers Ruth in early middle age with a sharp tongue and grace, a bright woman with agency and resources. Ruth lost her love young and raised two children on her own while managing a white folks' home northwest of Chester. She was as fierce as my mother's love for her—a gun-carrying, no-nonsense kind of lady. Her motto: *Don't start no rootin' and tootin', won't be no cuttin' and shootin'.*

But as tough as Ruth was, she was abundant in her outpourings—big blue crabs and Jersey Shore trips for her grands, regular feasts for Sunday dinners. Twenty years gone, my great-grandmother still has sway over my mom.

I can chart my mother's matrilineal line back eight generations. I always thought I'd lose our family footprints before my great-great-grandmother, Mary Gordy Townsend. Her mother, Eleanor Collins Gordy, was born before the Civil War, south of the

Mason-Dixon. I assumed, as I assume many Black Americans whose families haven't recently emigrated do, that my ancestors were enslaved. But after figuring out that Eleanor was listed in census records as "Ellen" and "Elenora" and "Elnora," I found her mother, Sarah Collins. The 1850 census data lists Sarah among the free inhabitants of Salisbury, Maryland, eleven years before the beginning of the war.

Recorded in residence with her was no man, but a woman about forty years her senior. I understand this woman to be my great-great-great-great-great-grandmother (with perhaps one more "great" in there, if there was a generation between her and Sarah): Hannah Collins. Hannah and Sarah lived with a smattering of children, including Eleanor, Mary's mother. These records root my mother's people two centuries deep on the Delmarva Peninsula—the mass of Delaware and slivers of Maryland and Virginia nestled between the Atlantic Ocean and the Chesapeake Bay.

Mary Gordy, born in the late 1880s, was the first to leave Maryland to move north after marrying. Across the border in Sussex County, Delaware, she gave birth to my great-grandmother Ruth, who recalled returning to Salisbury and surrounding areas to visit family. Mary and her husband moved their kids farther up the road to Chester, Pennsylvania, where Ruth gave birth to Sylvia, who gave birth to my mother, Chyrrea. My grandmother, mother, and I were all born in the same place—the same hospital, even. Our line became three generations of born Pennsylvanians even though my mother moved to Delaware before my birth—starting a slow return to the lands of her people.

***

Ruth always told my mom to "buy land by the water, 'cause God ain't making any more of it." So, during the Great Recession, when she was temporarily separated from my father, my mother purchased property in Horntown, Virginia—thirty miles from Salisbury. The three largely wooded acres sit inside a gated community called Corbin Hall. With just over one hundred lots, the neighborhood overlooks the Chincoteague Bay, which is separated by a skinny strip of islands from the Atlantic Ocean.

We lovingly call the place "the property," even though my mom owns her home in Delaware, as well. Its formal name (because naming is important when you're staking your claim): *Meiret*, an amalgamation of my brother's and my names. Although she hasn't built on the land, she goes to stay at the community's clubhouse annually. The large Georgian-style home also has a gym, a kitchen for events, a pool, and two apartments. Every couple of years, I stay there with her. Usually, it's the two of us.

In an Afrofuturist, multiverse way, I see our lives as Chyrrea and Chet'la running parallel to Hannah and Sarah: two sets of Black, Eastern-Shore-dwelling women whose names echo each other's in construction—sharing either similarly spelled beginnings or endings. But our circumstances are incomparable. Where we visit, they lived. Where they labored, we relax in luxury that feels triumphant.

My mother is a granddaughter of the Great Migration, second-generation northern on both sides of her family. Her elders left the land to work factory jobs, to run white people's houses, to serve in wards as nurses. In a single generation, they urbanized, decidedly pursuing upward mobility. Her paternal grandparents recounted tales of day laboring under the warm Florida sun from their Pennsylvania row home—their kitchen table stacked with produce from their small slip of yard nestled along its chain-link enclosure. Like Booker T. Washington, her grandparents valued both material resources and agricultural commitment, which they passed on to her.

At the first home my parents owned, my mom grew her own garden—cabbage, collards, and peppers. I can still taste the green bite of a vine-ripe tomato pulled from stem and consumed like an apple—masticating summer under my mandible. There are pictures of my elders standing among tall cribs of them stretched high by my swing set. We moved from that house when I was five, and while my mother still plants flowers, it has been a long time since she's worked the earth for food—her attentions directed elsewhere.

Chyrrea became a mother when she had my brother at sixteen. A driven young adult, she feared she wouldn't be able to deliver on the promise her family saw in her when she chose early parenthood. But she is nothing if not determined. At twenty-one, my parents met and married. At twenty-five, they had me. At twenty-six, they bought their first home—the one with the garden. At thirty, she wanted her future to look differently, completed her college degree in chemistry. She promptly applied to law school, from which she graduated at thirty-three, the same year she also promptly passed the bar. After she clerked for a Delaware Superior Court judge for a year, she became a chemical patent attorney at DuPont, creators of Tyvek and nylon. In twenty years, she went from teen mom to in-house legal counsel, all the while making sure her two kids were clothed and bathed and getting good grades. My mom is a superhuman, by which I mean I don't know how she did it—my father away in the service. I don't tell her this enough, probably because I've never felt like I would measure up.

As a snarky teen, I understood my mother's trajectory to be a fixation with status and station, which my baby rebel heart didn't want to participate in. But as she's come into focus with my softer eyes of adulthood, I understand how what she's done is, indeed, triumphant. I understand how much she was up against (white men assuming she was incompetent), how much she didn't want to become a statistic (never getting the degrees she sought), how much she wanted to live up to her family's high expectations (that she was a manifestation of hopes they'd had for generations). She, too, worried, as a middle child who had her first one young, that she wasn't enough; she, too, wanted to measure up. My mother, with the spirit of an Olympian, pole-vaulted over even her own imagination—now a VP at a life sciences company.

So when she's resting poolside at the property's clubhouse, I see not someone preoccupied with upward mobility, but a woman reaping the lush flora from all the seeds she's sown. We became her garden—the family, this life, her legacy. She holds us close so she can enjoy the bounty of her harvest.

Down at this bayside estate, I witness a different version of her—one that moves with more ease, less expediency. I used to think it was just the water that calmed her. But not even the sun's famous dive over the Cyclades islands in the Aegean Sea hits her the same way as the ambering blue sky over the Chincoteague Bay.

***

In bell hooks's essay "Touching the Earth," she writes that "generations of black folks who migrated north to escape life in the South returned down home in search of spiritual nourishment." My mother gets fed at "the property." It's not just that she's fulfilled a commandment from her grandmother. It's also that her now-gone father and sister helped her choose this land. Together, they drove three hours south to discuss lot sizes and shapes, to assess which trees might need to be cleared to build. Together, they decided on Lot 62: "the property"; *Meiret.* And once my mom had the deed in hand, she took her dad down to the pier to go fishing in the years his lungs started to fail. In the last months of my aunt's life, she and my mom sat in the clubhouse gliders, swapping stories of which my mom now is the only keeper. She still rocks in those chairs and talks to her sister, now ten years gone: "I did it, Gi"; "I know you're here with me."

At "the property," my mother can dip her hands in the waters of the near and distant past. And while she's unable to hold on to it for long, she enjoys the slip of it between her fingers. Awash in those unbreakable bonds that tether her to her grandmother, to her ancestors Sarah and Hannah, she's also buoyed by the fact that the waves of her will lap into the future. From a lounger she smiles wide, as she listens to my nephew hoot and holler, splashing in the pool after a full day baked by beach sun. She hopes the place will be in the family for generations.

Whenever I visit my friend Niya in Charlottesville, I am struck by her connection to the region. I don't know anyone else who is as tethered to a place as she is. Niya was born and raised in Albemarle County, Virginia, where her family has been since the 1870s. Before then, she can track them around central Virginia—Fluvanna, Louisa, and Orange Counties—back to specific plantations, in whose records her ancestors are listed among the inventories. Her entire life, save for two years, she's lived among her history.

On an unseasonably warm January afternoon, I stood with her in the yard behind her late grandmother's house, the one in which her father was raised with his siblings. Niya lived there while she finished her dissertation—replacing windows and restoring the floors, while tending to concord grapevines. In the middle of the grass, she gestured to the surrounding plots, telling me which elders lived where and when—explaining how that tract was sold off, but they got that one back. I listened with envy for the way she knows that landscape, only further amplified by her profession as a historian. With arms as wide as her sense of pride, she mapped for me a legacy of stewardship, fidelity, and communion. And as we slow sipped homemade moonshine, careful not to lose the whole day, I longed for how Niya *belongs* to central Virginia.

If I belong somewhere, it's to the Atlantic Ocean. I didn't know that truth lived in my marrow until the summer of 2020, when the pandemic kept me away from it. It wasn't the first time I hadn't dipped myself in the waters of my ancestors, but for the first time, I ached for it. I felt the fatigue and bruise from needing its nutrient-rich infusion. In the wake of the isolation, the violence, the loss, and the anxiety over the upcoming election, I craved the ocean I'd known as a toddler—the shush of its swells and its mute brown color imprinted on me. From it, I learned to respect both power and beauty. Sometimes, during that anemic summer, I'd submerge in bathwater and play wave sounds in my noise-canceling headphones. I'd visualize I was waterside and pray to be stilled.

For me, the Atlantic is where I feel the pull I imagine Niya feels to central Virginia, the one my mom perhaps feels for kin. But the closest I might get to that sensation on land is the Delmarva Peninsula, the "property." There, I watch wind-roiled grass wave and wander under a canopy of the loblolly trees. There, I listen to the rhythmic kiss of brackish water lapping against piling. There, I sit on the hot asphalt of the dock's parking lot and think, *One day, this will belong to me.*

But will I to it?

I wish I could end the essay here with the sun bright, face upturned to sky, body awash in water and light, as I bask in all my mother manifested. But my eyebrows furrow from the glare, and I have to look down at the ground.

While the gated community has a public name, like many estates, the subdivision declaration that established the neighborhood reveals its full one: Corbin Hall at the Chincoteague Plantation. Corbin: the name of a white man. Chincoteague: the name of Indigenous peoples removed from their land. Plantation: a demarcation of a farm embroiled in enslavement.

In the 1600s, the acreage was "owned" by Colonel Edmund Scarborough—a colonial official who savaged peoples of the Assateague and Pocomoke tribes. Although records say he was "given" the land, the Virginia House of Delegates biography of him describes how his disposition toward "Indians, Marylanders, Dutch, and Quakers ranged from aggressive to reprehensible." Based on this, I assume he procured the property through means of violence.

In the 1700s, the Corbin family purchased a tract of Scarborough's land. It proceeded to pass through its descendants like Colonel George Corbin, who built a house that was listed as a Virginia landmark until it burned down in 2000. When he died in 1797, he bequeathed to his daughter—well, only if she should marry and have a son—"the plantation." Some of their ancestors are still interred at Corbin Hall. George and my foremother Hannah would have lived at the same time, only thirty miles of green apart.

Laid bare for me in public records, these truths don't surprise but do disconcert me, the property's future steward. Settlers—who slaughtered its original stewards, who kidnapped, owned, and enslaved—became colonists. Colonists became Americans. South of the Mason-Dixon, Americans became Confederates only to become Americans again. The land my mother owns in Virginia has been sifted through those hands. But isn't that the nature of all property ownership in this country?

America: land of perpetual occupation, domination.

I don't dismay contemplating buying a condo in DC—a city named for a Founding Father who held people in bondage; a nation's capital built by enslaved laborers. Does Corbin Hall at the Chincoteague Plantation unsettle me because the history is a little less opaque? Because it is rendered plain in the community's name?

***

In 1662, the Colony of Virginia passed a law that declared ". . . that all children born in this country shall be held bond or free only according to the condition of the mother." The doctrine ensured that any child born of an enslaved woman—regardless of who the biological father might be, especially, say, if he were a white enslaver—would also be enslaved. The Virginia act spread through the British colonies. And in 1819, in *The Statutes at Large*, William Waller Hening added a Latin phrase after "mother": *partus sequitur ventrem*, meaning that which is born follows the womb.

I spend a lot of time thinking about inheritance, about epigenetics and intergenerational trauma, especially as I consider becoming a mom. What historical, chemical-level distress does my body harbor? What will permeate the placental barrier?

The prevalence of fibroids, benign uterine tumors, is three times higher among Black people presumed female at birth than it is among white people. According to the work of epidemiologist Dr. Anissa Vines, supported by the National Institute of Child Health and Human Development, fibroids and their pervasiveness are linked to stress and its severity. Many of my relatives have had hysterectomies to relieve the pain and flood of blood from fibroids. I'm currently monitoring the growth of mine, grateful they've found life outside my uterine cavity.

In our wombs, in our blood, we are still following the conditions of our mothers.

Born at least a couple of decades before the Act Prohibiting the Importation of Slaves in 1808, Great-Great-Great-Great-Great-(Great?)-Grandmother Hannah may have been the ancestor who survived my beloved ocean. Or it's possible that her mother was the one born on the continent of Africa. While the chance is slim, Hannah could have also been born free. Records document free Black people on the Eastern shore as early as the late seventeenth century. By the mid-nineteenth, when Hannah and Sarah lived on their own, Maryland had one of the largest populations of free Black people in a state that still held people in bondage. According to its archives, approximately 84,000 Black people were free either by birth or manumission in 1860—over 25,000 more than in Maryland's larger neighbor, Virginia.

I have years more of research to learn more about Hannah, to confirm she is the primogenitor I dream her to be—a free Black matriarch living in a intergenerational home, sowing seeds of liberated Black womanhood. So far, the records have revealed little. All I know: in 1860, she was near ninety and lived around mostly white neighbors. I know a bit more of Sarah, though. Census takers list her as head of household. Forty years younger than Hannah, Sarah had at least six children and worked as a laundress. In 1860, she also had twenty dollars' worth of personal property.

Neither woman was listed as having owned their home.

I know there's an act of reclamation inherent in land ownership as a Black American—denied our forty acres and a mule, redlined out of loans, displaced in service of "urban renewal." I know, for my mother, having property means beating the odds of what people presumed possible when she became a young mom. Through her, through Hannah and Sarah, we rework the legacy of *partus sequitur ventrem*.

When I squint my eyes against the glare of the sun, don my sunglasses, I can see its prismatic beauty—her harvest from soil near where her ancestors planted. In radiant polarized color, I envision what I could cultivate on this plot in honor of her, in honor of Sylvia, Ruth, Mary, Eleanor, Sarah, and Hannah.

I imagine building a wide, one-story home with a porch on the front and an east-facing primary. There's a solarium, a library for reading, and a run of rooms with nooks for meditation. There are bookshelves built into the walls and a western-facing kitchen that will be too hot in summers but warm in winter's late light lull. People I love and have chosen will congregate around the island counter as I cook dinner with produce pulled from my garden: basil, bell pepper, and mint; carrots and radishes. Each plucked from the types of dirt known to my foremothers. As I sliver collards and stew okra with tomatoes, I'll tell tale of the time my mom and I wandered a cemetery outside of Salisbury and stumbled across a headstone marked "Gordy"—my great-great-grandmother Mary's married name. I can see it even when the prism shifts, the rainbow filter diminishes.

I'll own the land but will still be beholden to zoning laws about setbacks and accessory structures, to an HOA with say over the removal of a community dog for excessive barking. I'll build a house to congregate my people, but all those big windows would need to be fortified against worsening hurricanes—glass and frames shipped from distances responsible for the climate change.

Ruth told her grandchild to buy land by the water, but what will I tell mine? Will I tell them to buy land in the hills? That god might not be making any more land by the water, but that he's clearly reclaiming it? Will I tell them owning the land where our people were bought and sold, where people were annihilated, is the closest I think we will come to reparations?

Will I tell them this is the cost of coming back home?

On Homing

In my hometown, on a bright May day, I watched a woman struggle to switch between her prescription glasses and shades outside of a Michaels art supply store. Her shopping cart—piled high with bags stuffed with yarn—inched forward. She tried to catch it with her foot, her hands otherwise occupied while she tucked a case beneath her left armpit and put on her sunglasses. There was mild distress in the woman's movements—her leg stretched as she tried to balance.

I laughed, but not at her.

Parking-lot Lady is who my friend Nikki sees whenever her partner Benae or I do the same routine: negotiating two pairs of spectacles and their cases as we step over street curbs and through store doors. Benae says Nikki doesn't understand because she's out here seeing for free, and I usually agree.

But watching Parking-lot Lady struggle, I understood what Nikki sees as we wrestle with different ways of seeing the world.

—

"In your leaving, you see your country," Joy Priest notes in her poem "American Honey."

In June 2022, I traveled to Rome with two other writers to conduct research for a potential collaboration. I served as our crude language guide, having studied Italian in college. Fragments and phrases flooded my tongue—the words for "toilet paper," the correct conjugation of past participles. Soon, choppy sentences turned to conversation, often smoothed by a glass of Cesanese. During mornings at cafés or nights having closing-time drinks, polite strangers would praise my pronunciation and ask: "*Di dove sei*?"—"Where are you from?"

My travel mates were quick to respond in English: "New York," where one lived currently, and "Florida," where the other grew up. And, I, well, I sunglass-fumbled.

In that moment, I had no permanent residence, having given up my place in central Pennsylvania almost a year earlier for research. I lived wherever I was: washing clothes at Airbnbs, retwisting my hair in hotel mirrors, filling prescriptions at local pharmacies.

I lived in the present.

But that was not what people were asking.

Different animals have different homing mechanisms to help them locate their primary habitats; some use topography and landmarks.

Like many people, I am from multiple places. I was born in Pennsylvania in the late eighties, did a two-year fellowship there in my twenties, and was employed as an assistant professor at Bucknell University. And even though the fact that I pronounce "water" like there's "wood" in the word decidedly places me from Delaware County, I've never affixed Pennsylvania with the label of "home."

Generally, I've settled on "the Mid-Atlantic" when people ask where I'm from, which has landed with varying degrees of success for my domestic and international interlocutors. I say I'm from the Chesapeake Bay watershed—raised on salt water, Maryland blue crabs, and the ease of interstate travel. And it's true.

Like an animal displaced after traversing a great distance, it's the region that I continue to return to.

When asked, "Where are you from?" I sometimes understand the question to be "Where do you call home?"

I could say Delaware; it's where both my parents currently reside. It's the state I've lived the longest: a collection of sixteen years over four decades. I grew up in New Castle County—Bear, Wilmington, Claymont. But I spent most of my time in Middletown, a place made "famous" by the single-screen theater featured in *Dead Poets Society*. My family moved there in 2000, right before I started seventh grade.

At the turn of that century, the town was cornfields and a stoplight—at least, that's how I remember it, having moved from the suburbs to farmlands. But Middletown and I both hit a kind of puberty at the same time. Rapid change came. Families and retirees moved below the C&D Canal to the less expensive property outside of the built-up boroughs of Wilmington. Recently shorn crops sent mice and deer skittering through construction and out past the town's limits. My family came shortly after the newly built high school, which promised to educate all the teens these new homes would bring. In that budding version of Middletown, on the cusp of its full blossom, my mother used to complain about having to cross a bridge and drive twenty minutes to buy socks and underwear.

Now, we reminisce about the Acme market the size of a bodega, about the Mexican spot with the fresh salsa, the loose tea shop. There are still a few small businesses in the historic downtown, but most, like Middletown Hardware, went out of business with the introduction of chains like Lowe's and Home Depot. The town now bursts well beyond its original four corners with cookie-cutter communities, two rival high schools, and fast-food franchises that outline strip malls. But even with Middletown's growth spurt—which continued to change its familiar landmarks and landscape—it was a place that I, for half my life, called home. Even though, it has never been a place where I've felt *at home*.

In 1984, Jordan Elgrably interviewed James Baldwin in the author's Saint Paul de Vence home in the south of France. In the conversation, Elgrably asked Baldwin, an expat for nearly forty years, about his relationship to the United States. He cited that, in 1968, Baldwin claimed to love America. Baldwin responded:

> "I still do . . . I think that it is a spiritual disaster to pretend that one doesn't love one's country. You may disapprove of it, you may be forced to leave it, you may live your whole life as a battle, yet I don't think you can escape it. There isn't any other place to go—you don't pull up your roots and put them down someplace else . . . [O]r, if you do, you'll be aware of precisely what it means, knowing that your real roots are always elsewhere."

"[W]illful rootlessness must be my state. Mostly, this suits me," Kiki Petrosino writes in her memoir, *Bright.*

In August 2021, I took a research leave from my job as a professor. I packed up my three-floor town house, put my belongings in storage, and hit the road. I wanted to know what "home" meant by briefly choosing a nomadic existence, by not having a ready-made answer for where it was.

I know.

What a privilege.

To choose to unhouse myself and to still know I have places to go.

But I hoped perpetual movement would prompt my mammalian homing device to click on, lead me to where I was supposed to knuckle down for the winter. Over the next eleven months, I clasped bluestem prairie grass in Illinois, smoothed my palm over driftwood in Washington, and held the small swell of a friend's baby belly outside of DC. I slept on air mattresses, couches, well-loved spare beds, and, when my body needed a break from friends' generosity, plush hotel pillow-tops.

By October, after only two months, I looked forward to my mother's house in Middletown: the pale green walls of my high school bedroom; the beachscape she'd painted that hung over my dresser; the way daybreak suffused the room in honey and amber. When I arrived, cranky and road-tired, I tumbled into a bath. Soaking in Epsom salts, surrounded by crystals and candles, I steeped in my own stew, lulled by lavender, by wave sounds churning through the Bluetooth.

But despite trying to breathe deep the curated calm, suck it into my lungs, I felt a hum in my chest—a quickening that clustered my neck.

I was in a home, a home I'd lived in for eight years, a home where I stored mementos—baby blankets and dolls, notes passed in high school. But I still wasn't *at home*—not in my body or in my spirit in a way that made my shoulders drop, set my heart aglow. I was just in the place my mother lived.

I wept about this.

—

Sometimes when people ask, "Where are you from?" I hear "Where, if anywhere, do you feel like you belong?"

—

Between 2006 and 2025, I lived in no apartment or house for longer than twenty-four months. Some of this was due to me picking up my life every time I had a new opportunity—a young writer trying to make a name for myself, trying to climb out of debt with a new configuration of employment. Some of this was due to restlessness, the need to try something different—vacillating between urban, rural, and suburban landscapes. Sometimes, I was just running.

For nearly two decades, I constantly replanted—moving myself into soil to which my system shocked, then steadied.

Or didn't.

—

Sea turtles and salmon use magnetoreception—the pull of Earth's molten iron core—as their navigation system.

—

I equated stasis to settling—be it a relationship, a job, or a place. If it didn't suit, I would relocate. I took pride in "growing where I was planted" temporarily, in unfurling my fronds to soak in sun then folding them up like the leaves of a prayer plant—conserving my energy, shielding myself from stressors. I'd do this open and close dance until my roots needed a new plot in which I hoped I could finally flourish.

But as I crept further into my thirties and invested more time trying to understand what I might, through moving, be trying to leave behind, I started to crave stasis. Something I never thought I wanted.

—

There are few places I feel at peace, like myself, other than submerged in a body of water bigger than a bathtub. But as I hungered for an anchor, for my life to find ocean floor around which the links in me could twist, I grew anxious. What if there is no place I can drop my full weight? And what could a constant free-float do to the child I hoped to create?

—

Where will my future child feel they are from?
 Where will they call home?
 Where will they feel like they belong?

Humans have no natural homing mechanisms.

During the first year of the COVID-19 pandemic, before I took the research leave from my job, I mostly stayed in my rented townhome in central Pennsylvania. I was lucky to have a two-bedroom, three-floor house to myself as friends and family renegotiated their relationships to together- and alone-ness. I woke up on the second floor, exercised and went to work on the third, and lounged on the first with a book or, more frequently, TV reruns.

My office window framed my days. I watched the seasons change between emails, meetings, and virtual teaching. The wet of winter exhaled into verdant green; a snake slithered the grass to bake in summer sun; COVID cases were on a steep incline. As the cornstalks climbed, with no one to come tend to them, I thought of Middletown and some of its former agriculture. I thought about how hungry I was to leave in those last years before graduating high school in 2006, listening to Story of the Year's song "Sidewalks." I often thought, during those lockdown months: *I feel the same way now as I did then.*

I entered less than ten public establishments that weren't medical facilities between March 2020 and March 2021, when I became fully vaccinated. I worried a lot about community spread and the medical attention I might (not) receive where I lived. As early as July 2020, passersby balked, accusing me of causing unnecessary worry when I wore my mask to take walks. At my favorite drive-up burger joint nestled next to the Susquehanna River, waitresses wore pins to explain they had health conditions that required them to breathe freely. I felt safest picking up grocery orders from my car and walking laps around the empty college campus.

By fall 2020, the main road down which I drove divided itself between Democratic and Republican candidates' signs. There was a single pride flag, one "racism has no home here" lawn sign, and a "silence is violence" poster in a window. In the weeks before the presidential election, a white friend asked if she could escort me on my errands after she saw a MAGA-clad gathering near the CVS parking lot. She asked the same when I went to vote—in a room with a woman wearing a "Blue Lives Matter" mask, a man without one, and a security guard watching the Republican candidate's speeches on his phone. All of them white.

In that sliver of the Keystone State, I lived in Middle America, the heart of the heartland that friends living just three hours away—in Philly, New York, DC—found hard to fathom. I lived in Abraham Lincoln's house divided.

—

In 1858, Lincoln won the Illinois Senate nomination against sitting senator Stephen A. Douglas. At the state's Republican convention, he delivered what we now call the House Divided Speech to convince people to vote for him over Douglas. Lincoln began the address as follows:

> "Mr. President and Gentlemen of the Convention.
>
> . . .
>
> We are now far into the fifth year, since a policy was initiated, with the *avowed* object, and *confident* promise, of putting an end to slavery agitation.

Under the operation of that policy, that agitation has not only, *not ceased*, but has *constantly augmented*.

In *my* opinion, it *will* not cease, until a *crisis* shall have been reached, and passed -

'A house divided against itself cannot stand.'

I believe this government cannot endure, permanently half *slave* and half *free*."

This oration occurred just three years before the start of the Civil War.

—

In 2020, my city-dwelling friends were stacked neatly in their condos, doom-scrolling on Twitter and *The New York Times*. While they spiraled about the pandemic and the failed state of the country, I lived in the America they feared would be a reality if the forty-fifth president were reelected. I pumped gas at the Sheetz alongside those who longed for the town's long-gone manufacturing; they wanted someone in power who prioritized them and their domestic concerns. Their surety in him shook me, as it did when I lived in Charlottesville during his first win. A colleague there smiled brightly the morning after that election. She was a first-time voter in her forties because she believed he could help deliver *her* American Dream. My hairs pricked at the possibility of what would unfold in that town less than a year later.

But in early 2021, as we saw him resist the transition of power, as we watched "proud Americans" take hold of the Capitol, as the January sixth insurrection exposed the heart of this nation, we all saw the cracks in its foundation—a version of

America we could no longer ignore, and one which 77 million people would support again in 2024.

In summer 2016, at the tail end of the Obama years, I took a near nine-hour drive from central Pennsylvania to northern Vermont for an artist residency. This may be nothing for people from big states. But I grew up in the second-smallest one, which you can drive tip to taint in the runtime of a Marvel movie. Since the mountains and ocean were never more than four hours from my mother's house, I'd longed to take a great American road trip—one where I could wind through the Sierra Nevada Forest for a full slab of day. Other people's stories—my father's, a former love's, my graduate school cohorts'—enticed me. They'd talk of Route 66 and roadside food stands, show pictures of themselves standing in the middle of an abandoned highway. That Vermont drive, in my mind, was going to serve as a precursor, an intro to what was possible.

But I was nervous.

Before the trip, I oscillated between my worries about truck-stop sex trafficking—of which my mother warned me to be wary—and small-town gas stations, after reading articles about Black people's modern-day, sundown town–type encounters. Before the trip, I straightened my short, natural hair despite the early July humidity. I wanted to be able to fit my otherwise full-bodied fro underneath a baseball cap. To be clear, I don't usually wear hats. To be clear, I had previously stopped at rest stops, lived in small towns. But I'd never done any of them on my own. So, before the trip, I aimed to construct an illusion of protection—selecting a non-suggestive travel outfit.

Humans may not know home in our bones, but we do have an instinct toward survival.

Even though there were stretches during my Vermont drive where I counted Confederate flags in Union states, I chided my anxiety as I passed shops with authentic Adirondack chairs and places to stop for fresh spring water.

I was fine. I was safe.

After a long day in the car, I arrived in Vermont unscathed, save for a migraine. I skipped most of the first-night festivities to take a sumatriptan and pass out in a stale room, hot from a midsummer heat wave.

That was July 3, 2016.

In the three days that followed, the news reported that police officers murdered Delrawn Small, Alton Sterling, and Philando Castile.

I was not fine. I was not safe.

I wanted to write about it then, but I couldn't. Instead, I ruminated. About these men. About Castile's girlfriend Diamond Reynolds and her daughter. About how they'd never recover from being in the car, live-witnessing his murder. About the nine-hour drive south that awaited me at the end of the month. About what a man asked me when I visited Italy for the first time in 2008:

"Are you one of the Americans?"

I am Black.

I am a Black American.

But am I one of the Americans?
And if so, what, if anything, does that citizenship mean?

Animals can find home but it doesn't protect them from predators.

In that 2020 summer when I yearned for travel, *The New York Times* published Tariro Mzezewa's article "2020 Is the Summer of the Road Trip. Unless You're Black." The article echoed what Brian Broome wrote in his July 2017 article for *The Root*: "I Want to Take the Great American Roadtrip Through the Heartland, But I'm Scared Because I'm, You Know, Black." In that piece, Broome writes of *The Negro Motorist Green Book*. It was a guide for Black travelers during the Jim Crow era created by postal worker Victor Hugo Green. Over fifty years after the last publication of the *Green Book* in 1966, Broome explains:

> "[Y]ou can't convince me with love nor money that we don't still need it. I watch the news. I've seen what goes on in the Dust Bowl states and, what good is the open road if it's not open to you? I do not want my trail to go missing somewhere in Adair County, Oklahoma."

But what happens in the Dust Bowl states also happens in Baltimore and New York, in Minneapolis and Ferguson.

Where are we from?
Where do we call home?
Where do we belong?

—

We are living through times that continue to be unprecedented, even as familiar stories get passed down through generations.

—

But "[t]here isn't any other place to go . . ." Baldwin declared.

—

Before the pandemic, I had planned to travel to Saint Paul de Vence in summer 2020 to write about Baldwin and his legacy, to see what it might be to follow in his footsteps. Instead, I sat on the third floor of my row home reading his *Paris Review* interview, in which he explained his decision to first move to Paris in 1948:

"It wasn't so much a matter of choosing France—it was a matter of getting out of America."

—

But there is no escape—of America, of prejudice.

Racism still touched the hem of the literary luminary's garment in the south of France—the landlady who feared him, found him tolerable, then acceptable, lovable, making him into one of "the good ones." And from across the sea, Baldwin wrote near constantly about the issues in this country.

—

Humans may not have a natural homing instinct, but we've built compasses to harness the earth's magnetic poles, drawn maps and taken photographs to trace new paths to keep us safe as we soldier forth.

In September 2021, a month after I embarked on my multi-week road trip, I drove from Cleveland, Ohio, to State College, Pennsylvania. I was headed to a colleague's house for dinner. Distracted by exhaustion, a headache, and a welcomed, warm embrace, I forgot to tell my family I arrived at my destination. While I was on the road, I checked in regularly. As someone who often misplaces my phone and doesn't bother to look for it for hours, I tried to be better with it in transit. I, too, didn't want to go missing.

After not getting a "made it" text, my mother called me. When she received no answer, she called my brother, who called me and received no answer. He called my father, who called me and received no answer and called my brother, who called me and then my mother. The loop continued—bubbling outward to a few friends. Hours later, I picked up my phone to see no fewer than forty text messages and calls. I looked at my colleague, a Black mother herself, and said, "I'm in trouble." She agreed.

Although Black women and girls amounted to approximately fifteen percent of all women and girls in the United States in 2020, we accounted for a third of those who were reported missing. Many of these women disappeared while making routine runs; meanwhile, I was solo driving through a series of states armed only with a Maglite. After the Cleveland to State College "incident," I started sharing my location. The "where" of me bouncing off satellites that twinkle in the night sky.

Indigo bunting birds bound south follow clusters of constellations.

"You may disapprove of it, you may be forced to leave it . . ." Baldwin remarked, but "[t]here isn't any other place to go . . ."

He left this country, understanding his roots to be elsewhere.

I stay, search, understand my roots are here—even as I struggle to decide in which soil they will thrive.

Part Two

WHERE DO YOU CALL HOME?

The Way Forward

What could end a country begins a mother.

—I.S. JONES

"Healing begins where the wound was made," Alice Walker writes in *The Way Forward Is with a Broken Heart.* And that seems simple. Right? It doesn't sound profound when we see spliced flesh on our thighs, the puncture of a mosquito bite. Of course, that's where healing starts. Our interior mechanisms promote immune responses to protect against infection. Biology bubbles in raised red patches, and we try to trust its magic. We wait for that translucent film, that initial scab over the gash, as our system sends its blood and wound-cleansing ooze, as it creates collagen and forms new tissue.

But what about the wounds we cannot touch? And I don't mean a broken heart—where we might be able to pinpoint when the relationship began to fall apart. I'm asking about the ones that are centuries deep and still festering.

In 1619, English colonists brought enslaved Africans to the shores of Virginia, beginning nearly 250 years of chattel slavery.

The ache of that initial injury still echoes throughout the country. I notice it daily—as I watch the news or prepare for a job interview, as I drive new streets or dress for the evening. I've never known anything different—born into an injured existence.

But as I started to decide whether I wanted to be a mother in my early thirties, I hated that this wound would be one my child would also have to attend to. Whereas I had white friends talk about the ecological impact of baby making, about climate change and the impending, and unfolding, crisis, I lived in the midst of a racial reality that had always been a crisis in this nation. I'd never known what it was like to feel truly *at home* in my homeland, the country of my birth. Does anyone who is not born white (and cis and straight, able-bodied and neurotypical) in America? Did I want to pass this on? And if not, how could I try to heal so perhaps the pain for my child wouldn't be so sharp?

I wasn't yet asking these questions when I boarded a flight to St. Louis, chasing the history of Black citizenship. But I did hope learning more could calm my internal quiver about my relationship to this place—that it would help me make my peace with bringing a Black child into this world—because to move forward, I often first move backward.

In 2018, the Delaware Art Museum participated in *Wilmington 1968*, a citywide acknowledgment of the weeklong spate of violence and civil unrest sparked by the assassination of Martin Luther King, Jr. In the wake of his murder, the nation boiled with anger and grief as people marched, looted, and burned cities. There was over twenty million dollars' worth of property damage alone in the country's capital. The government deployed more than 50,000 National Guardsmen to support local police in metropolitan areas. Eventually, when tensions simmered, Guardsmen retreated. But not in Wilmington. They stayed for nine months, at the instruction of the state's governor. This became the longest peacetime occupation of a US city in the country's history. A record that Wilmington still holds.

I'd been working for the museum for a little less than a year when these exhibitions debuted. In one of my early roles, I served as a Learning and Engagement assistant. In that position, I engaged in conversations about programming surrounding upcoming exhibitions and their legibility to our audiences. And I was eager to collaborate in the cultivation of the programs surrounding *Wilmington 1968*.

Participation in the commemoration was part of the museum's larger effort to connect with the city's Black citizens. Although the 2020 census estimated that fifty percent of Wilmington's 70,000-person population was Black, during my time there just a few years earlier, there seemed to be few Black museum regulars. Most of *us* who passed through the vestibule seemed to be employees and our associates, or those affiliated with a cocurricular charter school program. The museum wanted to change this and saw its involvement in the citywide acknowledgment as part of a multipronged approach to do so.

The curators planned three exhibitions for *Wilmington 1968*. The first was Hank Willis Thomas's *Black Survival Guide, or How to Live Through a Police Riot*, which he named after the thirteen-page manual in the Delaware Historical Society's collection that the artwork features. Each of the panels, which correspond to a page from the booklet, consist of a blown-up, black-and-white photo from the occupation on retroreflective vinyl—material generally used for street signs. Superimposed on each one is language from the eponymous guide: information about how a riot might unfold; suggestions for useful items to have on hand, like tourniquets and hand towels. This exhibition felt like the main event—perhaps because the museum commissioned it, perhaps because Thomas is renowned for his conceptual work, or perhaps because his was the only one of the three exhibitions by a Black artist.

Although the others centered photographs and renderings of Black Southerners and activists as well as descriptive labels written by Black leaders and community members, it struck me as strange that whiteness was still so prevalent in the art makers—a rendering of my history through the white gaze. This nagged at me—a hangnail snagging on the cotton of my dress—but the frustration didn't fully manifest—start to expose more tender flesh—until the L&E department discussed the Civil Rights Movement timeline that would accompany the exhibitions. My colleagues planned to start with 1955, with the Montgomery Bus Boycott. In December of that year, in Alabama, Rosa Parks refused to move to the back of a segregated bus; her arrest led to the protest that many mark as the start of the twentieth-century movement.

I suggested, instead, that we start at 1857, with the US Supreme Court ruling in the Dred Scott decision—a legal wound related to Black citizenship.

In 1846, Dred and Harriet Scott petitioned for their freedom in the slave state of Missouri. An 1807 statute popularized the practice, as it permitted people to sue for wrongful servitude. *Winny v. Whitesides*, an 1824 Missouri Supreme Court case, further fanned the freedom suit flames, establishing the "once free, always free" precedent. This meant people who could prove that they'd resided in Free States could petition for their manumission. Over three hundred Black people filed these suits during the first half of the nineteenth century in Missouri. About a third were successful, so the Scotts took their chances. Since they'd lived with their owner, John Emerson, in places where slavery was illegal, they thought they had a good case. The legal proceedings spanned the next eleven years.

An early complication: The courts couldn't determine who owned the couple. Was it Emerson's wife, Irene, who took ownership of the Scotts in 1843 after he died? Or Irene's father, Alexander Sanford, who leased the Scotts out for work? Ultimately, Irene's brother John Sanford undertook the lawsuit and presumed he could quickly get it dismissed. His argument: Scott had no right to sue. The basis: Black people, free or enslaved, were not citizens of Missouri. Without citizenship, Scott had no rights for which to fight. Sanford lost the case at the state level, so he appealed to the US Supreme Court. There, he doubled down on his position: Scott was not a citizen of Missouri; therefore, he was not a citizen of the United States. The Supreme Court agreed.

In Chief Justice Roger B. Taney's majority opinion for the *Scott v. Sandford* [*sic*] case, he wrote that Scott should remain enslaved, as he forfeited his rights to freedom when he left Free territories. Taney proceeded to explain his understanding of citizenship, citing a series of founding documents and previous cases. He argued that "the language used in the Declaration of Independence, show[s], that neither the class of persons who had been imported as slaves, nor their descendants, whether they had become free or not, were then acknowledged as a part of the people" and that Black people "had for more than a century before been regarded as beings . . . so far inferior, that they had no rights that the white man was bound to respect." For these reasons and others, he affirmed Sanford's claim: Black people—free or enslaved—were not citizens of the United States. This court decision was one of the catalysts of the Civil War.

When I taught first-year composition at a predominantly white institution in the early 2010s, my white students would sometimes turn in research papers clean of grammatical errors and want an A, even when their arguments were thin. When pressed on their claims, they'd say they couldn't find research to support their theses about how "inner city Black children are the reason for violence in professional basketball" or how "Disney's Snow White is an ideal role model for young girls." They'd litter their papers with unfounded assertions about how Black children are prone to aggression and how girls need to learn to cook and clean. As much as I challenged them to start the research process with a question and let the argument develop from what they discovered, I couldn't always cut through their desire to tell their versions of truth. In one class, a white student—who would go on to try to get me fired, suggesting I was unqualified—stated that "if racism still existed in America, then we wouldn't have *let* Obama run for a second term."

I learned a lot from them and their logic.

My students, like a lot of white America, have trouble accepting what both the archive and the present demonstrate. They prefer to bypass the "hard stuff." Fixated, instead, on "looking ahead," interested in "what we've overcome," they want to see how far *we've* come, because they can't bear the sight of how far *they* have to go. They refuse to see the wound—that the sutures will not hold—and their willful ignorance only makes it worse. No matter what, to heal a wound, we must be astute—mind it with the right mix of protection, oxygen, and medicines—to avoid infection, further damage, sepsis. Their inattention feeds the bacterial infection that is modern-day racism, which is at a fever pitch with its whitewashing of history, murders of children at play, and rhetoric dangerously close to the language from which Chief Justice Taney culled his argument.

A Civil Rights Movement timeline that starts with 1955 begins with the immune response, not the wound, with the attempt at recovery before understanding the root. This is the American way—"a pill to treat the ill" but not to address its cause, as an acupuncturist once said to me. The people of Montgomery, Alabama, didn't wake up one day and choose violence in the figurative sense, as the bus boycotts were a peaceful protest. But beginning the timeline with 1955 suggests that they did. White people treated Black people as, at best, second-class citizens for centuries. And in 1955, we simply were tired of it. I made this case in museum meetings, proposed other potential starting points: 1857, 1776, 1619.

The museum went with 1955; it was the easiest, most recognizable.

I was more incensed about this than I should have been. In fact, I was embarrassed by the strength of my dissent. I joked to my father one evening that I worried I showed up to museum meetings metaphorically waving my arms and saying "nigga,

nigga, nigga," before walking out. But as I huffed about the decision, I planted seeds for myself: one day, I would go to St. Louis, learn more about Scott, touch history's raw-edged wound in the courthouse of that first trial decision.

When I arrived in St. Louis three years later, in summer 2021, Pam Sanfilippo, the Chief of Museum Services and Interpretation at Gateway Arch National Park, pointed out details that I reveled in: the remnants of the original flooring, the historic courtroom bifurcated by a hall, the restoration work still to be done. I reached out to her after I started planning my trip to Missouri and learned the Old Courthouse was closed for renovations. I explained I wanted to work on an essay about Black citizenship, and she generously set up a call and scheduled a time to show me around. As I ran my fingers down a wall, fondled its gentle warp and waffle, I imagined the Scotts' waves of relief and anxiety as they oscillated between enslaved and free. As I touched the rough of wrought iron railings, the woodgrain of the circuit court doors, I hoped to be transported by the painted corridor, the way I was when I braced myself against the bricks where Sally Hemings once lived on Thomas Jefferson's plantation.

After four years of research about the woman who bore children by Jefferson, no experience was as transformative as treading the land she did during different seasons—touching the tips of frosted grass and listening to late summer's bug music. Being that immersed, that attentive, rendered tactile the intangible; I could see her cooking by fire, watching children play, swatting bugs in the heat of day. I sought that in the courthouse in St. Louis. I wanted to feel, in the walls, in the architecture, the heft of all for which the Scotts fought as I gave the life I wanted to cultivate some thought. Did I want partnership, a family, to keep writing in a place where my citizenship continued to feel, at times, precarious? But the time in which I lived was not more precarious than the one in which the Scotts did, one where I might be bought and sold and shipped states away from my loved ones.

Pam shook me from my interiority, as she described how the then in-progress renovation would allow for the National Park Service to construct galleries to reimagine the Scotts' story. She explained how they would provide a broader narrative—one beyond the case, one about who the Scotts were, who their family was. Lynne Jackson, the Scotts' great-great-granddaughter, would provide key perspectives. Ms. Jackson is a fixture in the St. Louis community—president and founder of the Dred Scott Heritage Foundation, responsible for the courthouse statue erected of her ancestors in 2012; she was integral to the new Gateway Arch National Park galleries. Since I wanted to know more about the Scotts, Pam arranged for the three of us to have lunch.

Across from Ms. Jackson, I jabbed at limp lettuce on my plate. Nervous, I lobbed loosely formed questions about the reinterpretation of the Scott exhibits. Ms. Jackson shared details not part of the public imagination: how her ancestors were in protective custody during the trial; how Harriet filed her own case in the event something happened to Dred; how their daughters were protected from a local madam intent on selling young women. Perhaps feeling badly for my obvious anxiety—and with the gentleness of an elder who could have grown kids older than me—Ms. Jackson pivoted to me, asked what I was hoping to gain from this trip to St. Louis.

I'd been asking myself the same question. Although I knew I wanted to deepen my relationship with the history of Black citizenship as I contemplated having a child of my own, I wasn't aware that I hoped St. Louis would render me more at peace with the legacy of disenfranchisement. But I didn't have language for the hurt, for the healing for which I searched. So instead, I told Ms. Jackson I wanted to better understand why I didn't feel like an American.

She briefly balked, and I felt a flash of embarrassment.

Although she didn't voice it, all I could imagine was that she was thinking: *After all that my*—our—*ancestors did?*

In the epilogue to *The Way Forward Is with a Broken Heart*, Alice Walker suggests that "the world cannot be healed in the abstract." You cannot just will away fascial lacerations, a bacterial infection. How was a trip to touch plaster going to fix this history? How could St. Louis heal an intergenerational injury?

In Dan Chiasson's *New Yorker* review of Claudia Rankine's *Citizen*, he explains how "the book explores the kinds of injustice that thrive when the illusion of justice is perfected." *Citizen* won all the awards, sparked conversations, was even read by a young Black woman, Johari Osayi Idusuyi, during a Republican presidential candidate's rally in 2015 (to much media frenzy). In the book, Rankine presents a series of microaggressions: being mistaken for another Black woman; the assumption that a Black person's check will bounce. *Citizen* demonstrates the quotidian nature of these infractions—a constant barrage as we go about our lives. These incidents are followed by a series of flawed, thin apologies from white people—an antihistamine for an allergic reaction in need of steroids.

In 2016, the Actors Studio in New York produced *A Man of His Time*—Kate Taney Billingsley's one-act play centered on a fictional, roadside diner meeting between Dred Scott and Supreme Court Justice Taney's descendants. Billingsley, the judge's great-great-great-great-niece, wrote it after several conversations with her family, the actual Taneys. Together, they discussed whether they should issue a formal apology to the Scotts. The play imagines how an attempted apology might go down.

A Man of His Time is filled with awkward tension and white-man missteps as Jim, a fictional Taney descendant, plays the broken "look how far we've come" and "Obama is our president" records. His apology to Walter, a fictional Scott descendant, is doled out with a gift: the late justice's gavel. Revolted by the thoughtlessness of the gesture, Walter responds: "You put the weapon in my hand."

I listened to a recording of the thirty-minute production on *Playing on Air*—an audio theater podcast with short-form shows by notable playwrights and performed by famous actors. This one featured the *Law & Order*–famous Sam Waterston and Tony-nominated stage actor John Douglas Thompson. As I stretched across a couch imagining what I heard, I cringed at the fictional Scott descendant delivering long, finger-wag monologues, knowing a white woman wrote them. I sat up straight when the *Playing on Air* recording censored a word I presumed to be "nigger."

Although the play's meeting was fictional, Billingsley brought the Scott and Taney families together in the real world—inviting Lynne Jackson and Charles Taney, the judge's great-great-grandnephew, for a talkback after a live show. This led to an actual apology, 160 years after the inciting incident. The Scott family accepted it.

In *Citizen*, Rankine writes: "Yes, and this is how you are a citizen: Come on. Let it go. Move on." And in the faux acquiescence of the book's speaker, we understand that these hollow apologies will never be enough.

An apology is an abstraction. Healing, the way forward, requires action.

A citizen is a resident legally recognized by a nation or state.

A citizen is a person entitled to rights and privileges of free persons.

A citizen is a member of a group, like a family, like a unit.

I understand that I am a citizen.

I understand why I don't feel I am.

I understand why Ms. Jackson and I had a different relationship to the word "citizenship" at lunch—across from each other in a moment of communion.

I am the textbook definition of an American citizen: codified by my birth certificate, under the Fourteenth Amendment, the Civil Rights Act, the Voting Rights Act, and the sacrifices of our shared ancestors. But there, at lunch, we sat twelve miles from where Darren Wilson murdered Michael Brown; he faced no charges for his crime. There was no retribution. This is why the word and legalese of citizenship feel as hollow as those *Citizen* apologies.

But I am grateful for the way Ms. Jackson startled. What I was doing *was* absurd. I'd gone to St. Louis to heal a wound, the one that declared my people not citizens. But St. Louis didn't do that to us. The US government did. The hallowed halls and frescoed ceiling of that courthouse did see Scott as a citizen, even if briefly. And that place couldn't atone for the disenfranchisement that pre- and post-dated it, for the violence of many generations. The Black American body politic is riddled with lesions from centuries of injury. There were so many wounds, and there was no singular site that we could suture. So, what could be healing?

In 1971, Aesthetic Dynamics, Inc.—a Delaware-based, Black-operated arts organization—exhibited more than 130 works by more than sixty Black artists. The show, *Afro-American Images*, included hometown heroes like Edward Loper Sr. and Jr., as well as other nationally recognized artists like Faith Ringgold and Hale Woodruff. Percy Ricks, the organization's founder, contacted the Delaware Art Museum about featuring the show; they ignored him.

In 2018, the same year as the commemorative *Wilmington 1968* exhibits, one of the Delaware Art Museum's curators worked to right that decades-old wrong. She, in collaboration with Aesthetic Dynamics, planned a fiftieth-anniversary restaging of *Afro-American Images* at the museum, celebrating its oft overlooked role in the Black Arts Movement and "ensur[ing] the wrongs of the past aren't perpetuated today." I didn't know this was in the works when I was railing about timelines. The Delaware Art Museum couldn't atone for the sins of US history, but they could attempt to atone for their own—debriding the wound they'd caused.

At the *Afro-American Images 2021* opening, the joy in the room was palpable in the laughs and affirmative *mmmmms* of the members of the Aesthetic Dynamics organization and the Black community. The museum now has regular programming that streams us in: Black '90s film screenings; celebrations of hip-hop culture featuring Flavor Flav. The late Percy Ricks's dream, to laud Black art in the state's art institution, finally realized. In a gallery at the show's opening, which beamed a family reunion–style energy, I asked myself, *Is this healing?*

Despite the 1857 Supreme Court decision denying Black people citizenship, the Scotts gained their freedom that same year. When John Sanford was institutionalized, Irene and her new husband, a Massachusetts Congressman opposed to slavery, regained ownership of the Scotts. The couple sold Dred and Harriet back to the Blow family, who'd owned Scott before Irene's first husband. The Blows—who maintained a deep care for the couple, including providing financial resources for lawyers—helped the Scotts secure their freedom. Dred Scott died from tuberculosis a year later—of all days, on the anniversary of the signing of the US Constitution. *We the people . . .*

I am beginning to understand that the way forward means I must accept that we can apply salves and medicines, but nothing may lead to a full recovery. Sometimes infections, or the body in stress, can trigger autoimmune diseases—ones in which the body overresponds to itself, as it would to a foreign agent like a virus, causing inflammation and damage. Although some autoimmune disorders—like giant cell myocarditis, which inflames the heart's muscles—can be fatal, most are treatable; none have a cure.

In Meghan O'Rourke's *The Invisible Kingdom: Reimagining Chronic Illness*, she writes that to have a chronic illness "is not only to have a disease that you have to manage, but . . . a story that many people refuse to hear—because it's deeply unsatisfying, full of fits and starts, anger, resentment, chasms of unruly need." I remind myself of this when a white neighbor asks me if I've ever *actually* experienced racism. I remind myself of this after the 2024 election, when the nation votes again for a man who is representative of a larger condition.

In a place, in a country, where the prognosis will never be total rehabilitation, in which sick will forever be our modus, should I even be looking toward what it might mean to be healed?

Alice Walker's book isn't called *The Way Forward Is with a* Healed *Heart*. Instead, the title acknowledges the irreparability, the constancy of that reality. As someone with autoimmune conditions, you'd think I know that looking for a singular cure is a fool's errand. You'd think I know mitigation is a lifestyle, a commitment to not succumbing to the tribulations. Why would I think my relationship to this country would be any different?

***

Autoimmune disorders are difficult to diagnose and treat. When patients haven't responded to other treatments, doctors suggest biologics. These drugs, which target and block specific immune responses, are made from living organisms and cells.

So what would it mean to heal from within myself with the introduction of new cells, a new organism? To have a baby. To do it despite my fears about rearing them in a country where the fact that our lives matter is, to some, an arguable thesis as opposed to a fact.

After St. Louis, I started to wonder what could be more radical than to thrive, to prioritize creating life, in a place that doesn't want me to survive?

Camille T. Dungy writes that her "poems are informed by displacement and oppression, but they are also formed by peace, by self-possession."

Could a child born of me, in this country, not only be informed by displacement and oppression, but formed by a kind of peace, of self-possession? Could it invoke a kind of healing? One in the new flesh sense—not in the abstract.

Heart in the Heartland

heartland (noun)

1. the central states of the United States, regarded as representing traditional social attitudes and moderately conservative politics

Ex. 1: Kansas City, Missouri (February 2024)

In the hotel desk, I find the Book of Mormon. Auntie Em, I must be in Kansas.

Which I'm not. I'm just over the border in a Missouri Marriott, its founding family connected to the Church of Latter-day Saints prior to the company's inception. But it has been a while since I've cracked open a drawer to discover a book of scripture, especially one other than the King James Version I was raised on. Here, the religious text slides forward with force while I search for another pen—mine ran out in the middle of this telehealth appointment.

Four years ago in Lewisburg, Pennsylvania, my therapist and I discussed my desire to be a parent. She asked if I was waiting to be partnered. And I said no. She paused and asked what I was waiting for, then. I didn't have an answer. Not yet. But then, I saw the ways in which I wanted to rearrange the bits of tile that made up my life's mosaic. As I started to shift them—leaving a job and place that didn't serve me, managing my health, establishing a community supportive of my next chapter—the image settled on something I admired for myself.

And now, I am here in a hotel room in Kansas City, looking for a fresh pen to take notes about fertility clinics, doctors, and next steps. Nearly two years deep into a lupus diagnosis, fifteen years into celiac, and twenty years into chronic joint pain, I am used to this—the appointments where I take copious notes, only to have more questions later. But, to be fair, I didn't think this call would come while I traveled for a conference—an annual gathering of thousands of writers. I'd requested the appointment a week earlier, but the fertility clinic said it was experiencing a high call volume, so I figured I'd have a few weeks to collect myself as I launched into this potential future. Before I scheduled this, I thought I'd spend today driving four hours west. Destination: the center of the contiguous United States; Lebanon, Kansas.

It's fitting that the heart of the lower forty-eight should bear that name. "Lebanon" is one of the most popular nomenclatures for a city, town, or census-designated place in the country, with almost as many as there are states. Most of them are east of the Mississippi. Similar to places like "New Hampshire" and "New England," "Lebanon" is a vestige of the Old World, dates back to colonial America.

In 2016, Fadi BouKaram, a Lebanese tech consultant turned photographer, decided to travel through the United States' Lebanons. The quest commenced when, in search of a map of his home country, he discovered a town that shared its name in Oregon, where he lived; then, in other states. A few weeks before the presidential election, he trekked east from California to visit each, to learn more about them. His archival research revealed the naming convention connected to the Puritans and the Bible; they preferred the Geneva version:

> The righteous shall flourish like a palm tree; *and* shall grow like a cedar in Lebanon.
>
> —PSALMS 92:12

> The glory of Lebanon shall come unto thee, the fir tree, the elm and the box tree together to beautify the place of my Sanctuary.
>
> —ISAIAH 60:13

Before the fall of the Ottoman Empire and the post–World War II establishment of the country, "Lebanon" referred to a mountain range and an area known for its white-capped peaks and fruitful forests in the Middle East. This incarnation of the word appears over seventy times in the Old Testament. It is a sacred and holy land; its cedar trees exalted.

BouKaram explained that "the [Puritan] settlers, would see a forest and think: 'Those are cedar trees,' even though the cedars of Lebanon didn't exist in the New World . . . [A]nd say: 'Let's call this place Lebanon.'" He joked that as expansionists moved farther west, they were less religious, so the name fell out of fashion. But still, "Lebanon" found its way into newer tracts of the country—worming north to south in Tornado Alley states.

In the Bible, Lebanon was conquered, a land over which men like Joshua reigned in the Lord's name:

> All the places whereon the soles of your feet shall tread, shall be yours: your coast shall be from the wilderness and from Lebanon, and from the River *even* the river Perath, unto the uttermost Sea.
>
> —DEUTERONOMY 11:24

Etymologically, the word "Lebanon" is also related to *laban*, which is related to the root of *lbn*: of, or related to whiteness—and, by extension, a kind of purity. These roots, origins, and derivations support America's integral ideals: prosperity, whiteness, and dominion. It makes sense, then, that the heart of the heartland bears this name.

***

I only want to go to this particular Lebanon to say I've been to the center of the lower forty-eight, to Kansas—one more state to cross off my own quest to visit all fifty before age fifty. Another goal, like parenthood, I've set for myself. But I'm beginning to tire of arriving new places. Ready, after fifteen years, to move at a slower pace, one that doesn't dull the ache of restlessness through movement.

In Molly McCully Brown's "If You Are Permanently Lost," she writes, "Sometimes I think I've made myself into a constant traveler as a mechanism of defense . . . I'd rather be a stranger, transitory and alone, because of something I decided than as a consequence of something in me, some lack that proves again and again what a damaged animal I am." I may not have a clear sense of home, where to rest my bones, but I do want to begin to love my damaged animal—my mammal with no homing mechanism. Because I know that others, too, search the night sky without answers. That those truths and my desire to be grounded aren't incongruous.

That's why I'm on the phone with the fertility clinic, beginning a conversation about a future I'm afraid to want in this place with whiteness at its center.

Ex. 2: Nashville, Tennessee (July 2022)

From the floor, I watch Erica stuff her breast into M's mouth—agape with hungry wails, sucking up air instead of milk. She rocks in the glider until he settles, nuzzles into her, and starts to audibly nurse. The noise is satisfying to untrained ears, the wet smack of a joyful feed, but the sound, I learn, is indicative of the type of latch he has. She tells me this as she football-palms him—his infant back slack as his abdomen flexes. He's three months old now; she goes back to work soon.

A decade earlier, Erica and I lived in tight-quartered DC apartments. We went to bottomless brunches we charged to our credit cards—spending four hours bellied up to bars for mimosas and tapas. I'm still paying off debt from those days, when I loved a man who was not good for me, and she was dating the man she would marry. Now, Erica lives in this three-bed rancher with her husband and M, who eats in his jungle-themed nursery. Sometimes I look at her life, full and beautiful, and see my own lack.

Erica tells me she's not sure how I'll do this alone: make and take care of a human. And I know she means this in love, with concern. Everyone does. They say, "I don't know how you [insert things I do as a single person in her thirties] alone," with soft-scrunched eyebrows and a touch on the arm. But what I also hear people telling themselves, when they look at me with a tinge of relief, is that this hard thing they're doing could be harder. Maybe that's just my anxiety. Maybe I'm projecting. In reality, I do the same, looking at people who hadn't planned to child-rear solo but discover their partners unfit for the job. Her spouse isn't this way. He's stretched on the floor, like me, as Erica chest-feeds, before he gets up to walk the dog down their tree-shaded street.

Erica's happy but somewhat isolated here in Nashville, her hometown. She moved from New York City to have M—currently palming her back, pads of fingers pressed against her full breast. Most of her childhood friends, like her, moved elsewhere. And the ones who stayed grew in ways that their relationships couldn't sustain. But moving back home was the right decision. M will grow up with a lush garden, hands in dirt that will produce pansies that tickle his nose and peppers he'll pick for dinner. He'll ride his bike down streets that will become familiar for their cracks and divots. This is the vision they have for their family.

Erica is happy. But even when we have what we envision, it's never without complication. In the song "Thank Goodness" from the musical *Wicked*, Glinda the Good Witch grapples with how happiness isn't seamless, how there are things she's lost on the journey to what she thinks she's always wanted, how there are costs she hadn't anticipated. While everyone around her celebrates her good fortune, Glinda suffers in silence, radiating cheer.

And while Erica and I are both familiar with the dead-eyed-smile energy of "Thank Goodness," we don't fake it with each other, launching into real talk with an emphatic *Girl*. Her transition to motherhood is no different. We talk the general things: birth story and isolation and the shit we thought our parents would stop doing. But we also talk specifics.

She's still wounded from the delivery and the treatment she received when she was heavily drugged, when M was a knot of new flesh that had just exited her. She, a Chinese American woman, became mother to a son with Black, white, and Chinese heritage. With his birth, she arrived at a new intersection of racism, the crossroads where medical racism meets Blackness.

From the floor, I prop myself up, touch Erica's arm; M continues to suckle.

Ex. 3: Geneva, Illinois (March 2022)

This is the second time I'm visiting Molly in Geneva, her hometown. I'm here to see *Tosca* with her at the Lyric Opera of Chicago. This is a redo visit from when I came to her place last year and spent most of the time sick. A weekend rolled into a Wednesday as I fought a fever and gastrointestinal upset; I'm talking yellow-water backdoor explosions when bright bile wasn't erupting from my nose and mouth.

That was in August 2021, when many of us were just taking our first steps back into the world after that initial, fogged pandemic year. I'd decided to embark on a two-month road trip; Geneva was my sixth stop in two weeks. As I'd tiptoed—or maybe, more accurately, sprinted—back into life post-lockdown, I traveled with a thermometer. After a year of being Bubble-Wrapped in my apartment, I assumed coronavirus would find me as I snaked through states. And there I was in Molly's house, watching my temp creep up.

I met Molly back east in Lewisburg, Pennsylvania, years earlier, when we were tied to a town that would eventually break us both. Geneva reminds me a lot of that place. It is bigger than Lewisburg, but both are situated near rivers and boast small-town charm: chocolatiers and vintage shops; flowers and brick sidewalks maintained by the money-thick pockets of its residents.

The day before the sickness set in, Molly and I walked a prairie preserve, where wildflowers drooped heavy-headed. We had drinks on a patio before our shared steak frites dinner. While I sipped my wine, I watched the polo-and-sunglassed masses stroll by. They reminded me of the white people with whom I'd gone to college, who, even in sweatpants, donned pearls and popped collars. Often these "charmed" towns are sparsely melanated, feel a little segregation-light, so I'm skeptical of the smiles and polite nods from passersby.

In the height of the Jim Crow era, Illinois had more sundown towns than any other US state. I thought about the remnants of this in the whiteness I experienced all day—at the grocery, on our walks, at dinner. But while we were on the patio, a family who appeared to be of South Asian descent walked down the street. As they passed, a small child bounding ahead, I could feel a slight reset in my chest, the space growing between my ears and shoulders. Molly and I exchanged a smile. She clocked it, as well. After that, we saw a few more people I'd classify as part of the global majority—a weird safety bean-counting process I'd taken to in my travels.

When I woke the next day, I was surprised to be hungover after two glasses of wine. After muscling through breakfast and tumbling into a mid-morning nap, my body shivered under blankets. I took my temperature: *101.1*. Molly and I weighed the pros and cons of going to the doctor. This was before everyone had rapid tests on hand, so when you thought you had COVID, you still had to go get nasal-swabbed somewhere. *101.7*. If it wasn't coronavirus—which seemed unlikely, because GI activity and the fever were my primary symptoms—then going to a hospital or testing center could expose us. And if it *was* COVID, then Molly and I would be separated. *102*. As the day went on, no matter what I did, my fever continued to click upward: *102.2*. We agreed we wouldn't go anywhere unless my fever crested *103*; Google informed us this was when we should consult a doctor.

I soaked in warm baths in her deep tub, and Molly dropped

off water and broth, double masked and gloved. I took Tylenol with Gatorade, nibbled on white rice, and threw it all back up as I firehosed the toilet bowl. I slipped in and out of consciousness from febrile naps, which made Molly nervous about the baths. We communicated at least once an hour when I was up, which wasn't often. She didn't sleep. We both cried. When my parents called, I let my phone roll to voicemail.

What Molly and I didn't say was how scared we were to be separated at a hospital. We'd read all the stories of people parting with their loved ones at triage for what they didn't know would be the last time. We'd read about doctors having to choose who got ventilators. We'd known about white doctors' biases when it came to Black suffering. Even as my teeth began to ache from the clench and chatter of my temp, I waited to take it until she prompted a check via text. *102.7*. Sometime after ten P.M., I fell into a long-night slumber, able to quiet my quivering abdomen for several hours. I woke to her message: *Temp check?*

The year before this, I had discovered lumps in both my armpits. I spent weeks unwell with worry, awaiting scans and a biopsy. Even though the ultrasounds deemed the masses swollen lymph nodes and the biopsy confirmed their swelling not malignant, I was convinced something other than necrotizing lymphadenitis, which my doctors seem unbothered by, was the culprit. This made me particularly scared to catch COVID.

For the first five years of our friendship, Molly had unexplained cluster headaches that clustered her weeks. For most of those years, we joked about how we both might die young. But during that time, she pursued two master's degrees. And while off at poem school, she learned a critical vitamin-D deficiency was the cause of everything. The cluster headaches disappeared; she's going on four years.

We'd quietly rumbled through health storms together: both of us laughing off potential diagnoses and death sentences over rosemary salt–crusted steak and Beaujolais. There are few friends I can do this with. That I can look at and laugh when I say twenty could have been middle age. But despite the ubiquitous existential dread, Molly and I are fairly close-lipped about health-related specifics until prompted by the other for an update. There is a general understanding between two people for whom our individual anxieties are such that our arms cannot hold the weight of someone else's worry.

In those tense twelve hours in Molly's house, despite oscillating between Tylenol and Advil, my temp kept climbing closer to our *103* boundary. It was a test of friendship for her to be in it with me, to be in this full-body fear that I showed next to no one. I'd cried in front of her before. Sure. But not because I was scared. I rarely give people access to the type of tears that leave my eyes so swollen, they look as if they could be deflated by a pin prick. I've saved this for a select few aside from my parents.

In that stretch where I slept, Molly, like the parent of a newborn, cracked open my door to listen for the hum of me. We were new to this, but we had to let go of the artifice. By morning, when I woke to her temp-check message, I felt like I'd been run over—plastered against the mattress in a mix of lethargy and sweat. I slid the thermometer in my mouth: *102.1*, I texted. She replied: *Good.* I sipped fresh bedside water and, an hour later, I was still able to keep it and a few crackers down. I reported this, as well. She responded: *YAY!!*

We celebrated the victory later that night by me leaving the room—masked—to make sure I could take a lap around the house. We were still worried about COVID. But I breathed easily and started to crawl out from what we assumed was a stomach bug. Once I was better, two to three days later, we decided I'd come back in March to go to the opera with her.

And now I'm here on this do-over trip, and we're bitching about the regular things—houses, jobs, changes to come—over mussels and grilled octopus in downtown Chicago. We walk against the winter wind before we file into the theater to hear Michelle Bradley vibrate the walls with her arias. This is my first time at the opera, so I'm excited, tipped forward like an eager toddler, but also overstuffed from dinner—distracted by how my skirt chafes my stomach. Still I enjoy the lilt and tilt of Bradley's voice.

As we tumble back into the night, Molly and I are both grateful for the crisp chill, our bodies heated with delight. On the ride back to Geneva, we joke about the horror of "last time." We laugh in the way where we don't know if the tears that brim our eyes will shift to sobs. I worry if she can drive in this joyful, wet-eyed way. And just as she calms, she remembers how I was willing to pack myself up and drive to a hotel to protect her from me when my temp was still south of 102. We barrel back into laughter.

When we return to Geneva after our night of merriment, we plan for rest, rom-coms, and grilling out the next day. I fall asleep in a bed not damp with my sick, relieved for this visit to be different.

But in the morning, I wake with chills and aches, the singe in my throat of stomach acid.

heartland (noun)

2. a region that is especially important to or associated with a particular activity, organization, or ideology

Ex. 1: Lewisburg, Pennsylvania (April 2024)

I thought Bucknell University could be my chance at the American Dream. I first moved to Lewisburg, Pennsylvania, in 2014 for a fellowship at the institution to complete my first book. Disillusioned from four years in DC working sixty-hour weeks to make just over $40K, I was excited to move to Pennsylvania. It was a town where I could walk to the CVS or to the Art Deco theater to watch *Still Alice*, crying into a slim bucket of popcorn drizzled with real butter. The type of town in a Hallmark film where a big-city writer moves and finds themselves endeared to.

Even though I would often play the "had I seen any Black people today?" game, I nestled into this town through which four-car trains would crawl. I was living a big life in a small place—knowing the names of the art store owners, going every Wednesday to the farmer's market, and eating meals with the type of loved ones the city kept too busy to gather regularly. The days lingered as long as the winters, as I read in rare patches of sun, attended poetry events, and went for wooded walks. When my two-year fellowship ended in 2016, I cried as I drove off into an uncertain future.

When I returned to Bucknell a few years later to accept my first tenure-track job as a professor, I still hoped Lewisburg would offer me the opportunity to pursue my American Dream. I imagined an upper-middle-class existence with a cushy savings, a home of my own with a yard. My other first-year colleagues built this for themselves while they taught five classes a year and attended department gatherings, ensuring their university commitments remained low so they could spend the next six years focused on tenure. Meanwhile, I taught three classes and directed the Stadler Center for Poetry & Literary Arts—a nationally recognized center for creative writing; it was home to a fellowship, a residency, a literary magazine, a summer program, and a reading series. In my first year, I also served on the university's Art Council as well as the College of Arts & Sciences Strategic Planning Committee at the request of my associate dean, while maintaining my commitments as faculty in the creative writing program and English department.

American Dream (noun)

1. the idea that every citizen should have equal opportunity to achieve success and prosperity through hard work, determination, and initiative

Turns out, Bucknell was the American Dream for some, but not for me—one of less than a dozen Black women on the faculty. As I worked to prove I was enough, as I advocated for more support, I was told my predecessors had done my job with less retorts. I wrote in fits and starts; my vision of an idyllic, small-town writing life a wisp disappearing in Lewisburg's meager morning light.

My body told me this couldn't go on long, as physical and mental symptoms manifested: joint pain that lit fires in my lower extremities; migraines that clouded my days; and a bout of depression that prompted my therapist to offer to lend me her family dog, which looked like the one my family had put down a year earlier. The university's tendrils of infection snaked through my system, purpling my veins. And it wasn't just the inequity of labor.

In a one-on-one with my associate dean, my vocal cords quivered while I tried to explain why I no longer wanted to participate in certain types of meetings. I was skeeved by the senior colleague who sent me a private Zoom message telling me I was stunning; enraged by another who called me and another Black woman faculty member "antagonistic." The general recommendation from others in the academy, in response to these two white men: muscle through—especially since I would be on sabbatical, a paid university leave for scholarly productivity, soon. I deserved tenure; this was the pathway to it.

In April 2022, in breach of contract, I quit my job while on sabbatical. Since publication is a core tenet of most academic jobs, my sabbatical was timed to support travel and research for a book. I could take a semester off at full pay or receive half my salary to take a year. I opted for the latter. Some universities have provisions that state that a faculty member must return for a full year after that type of leave or pay back the salary; Bucknell is one of them.

I thought, foolishly, that perhaps the university would release me with ease. I'd worked more for my institution during my research leave than other junior colleagues did. I continued to help the center I directed by serving on committees, moderating an intercollegiate event in collaboration with two other liberal arts institutions, and assisting with plans for the upcoming reading series. These acts of service didn't matter. Bucknell required me to repay part of my salary for the right to resign. So, I did. I signed tens of thousands of dollars away to them in defeat and exhaustion, depleting the cushion I'd built working twelve-hour days through the thick of the pandemic. I also returned to Bucknell for a semester to lower the amount I owed and to smooth the transition. When classes were done and the final payment was withdrawn that December after my one-term return, I drove away unsure if I'd ever come back, crying different tears than the ones I had in 2016. The Dream I once thought possible flame-engulfed in my rearview mirror.

In those first post-Lewisburg months after the second move, I could still feel the heat of its infection. Bucknell was a place I so badly wanted to make a place I could stay, not just for me, but for the students I taught who weren't a part of the Audi-driving, boat shoe–wearing masses. But my body and brain kept asking me why I wanted to stay in a place that could not conceive of me in its imagination.

Couldn't I ask the same thing of this country?

Now, a year and a half after leaving that cold December, I pass through Lewisburg to see people. I thought I'd come back sooner, but I couldn't, not until I'd recovered some of what was lost—including my money, which was reimbursed to me after two Black women administrators made a case that I had been unjustly made to pay. When refunded funds hit my bank account, a wound vac started to siphon the residual bits of Bucknell's disease. And after a year in DC of having monthly Sunday dinners with friends and date nights with my beloveds, after a year of new doctors nursing my autoimmunes into remission, I've fallen back into the rhythm of myself: writing long swathes of the day, dancing in my kitchen. Friends say they can see the way the illness is leaving me, and they aren't talking about the lupus—with which I was diagnosed the same April I decided to leave Lewisburg.

As I turned back into the town earlier today, I remained skeptical—worried its lingering poison might still surge beneath my skin. It doesn't. Clouds cling to skies slow to let go of winter as I drive to the local food store for CBD oil and thirty miles north for a decaf latte dappled with lavender. I do this all without map or mindfulness. There's an ease to this sort of knowing, one I used to equate with home. But now I am beginning to understand the difference between a place being home and a place being familiar; the difference between ease and actual belonging.

For a decade, since I first moved there in 2014, Lewisburg figured prominently in my conception of the American Dream. That was only amplified by the ways in which I understood it to be inaccessible to me as a Black woman in this country, killing myself to succeed at that university. But here, with my shoes briefly brushing its streets as I move in and out of the homes of friends who still live here, I know I don't need to dream of this place, that college, that I don't need to dream a dream that doesn't dream of me.

As the sun dips its toe into my side-view mirror, I sigh, relieved to longer be deluded by this place's illusions.

Ex. 2: Paradise Valley, Arizona (May 2022)

As I sit poolside, the ice in my Nalgene turns to liquid, but the bottle never perspires. I've heard dry heat hits different. But it's 102 degrees, and I'm still hot. Overheated, in fact.

At the Sanctuary Spa, Kaya, Sayers, and I nap, hydrate, and chat under white umbrellas and matching daybeds. We woke up at five A.M. to hop on treadmills and lift weights before breakfast, before heading to the spa for facials and massages. I left the morning endorphin-drunk from the caretaking of my massage therapists—particularly the one who made sure my cervical spine was aligned, placing rolled towels underneath my shoulders before she started her work. After two hours of rubdowns and rain sounds, I toddled through the quiet spaces to locate Kaya and Sayers. We gushed in hushed tones about our respective treatments.

Kaya and I are the only Black people here, the only people of color outside of one or two others working. We sometimes encounter this on our annual birthday trips, where we traipse through cities for good gluten-free food and booze. Two autoimmune zoos, we're often trying to wrangle the wildlife of our bodies, but we feed them well on these birthday expeditions—living our best bougie Black girl lives. There were the crab cake benedicts in Denver, the Black-owned Merlots in Napa, and the pounds of fresh pasta in New York.

In Arizona, we've enjoyed fried cheese curds and five-course meals paired with wine, amuse-bouche, and dessert. The Southwestern landscape is foreign to both of us East Coasters—no ocean or deciduous lush to encompass us. And it's not just the heat; it's the dust devils that whip across tan, arid land dotted in cactus green. But like with the altitude in Colorado, we appreciate, adjust.

After our massages, we venture out to the pool to lounge and lunch. Another spa-goer soon appears in the water and strikes up a conversation. I ask the woman if she is from Phoenix, but she corrects me. "Scottsdale," she responds at a curt clip. I clock her insistence. Understand there must be a difference, wonder if it is akin to "the DMV" versus "DC." But I don't really care as I float, the water warm, simmering from sun.

I am tired from the massage-related toxin release and dehydration. So I'm already depleted when a white man asks Kaya and me if we're twins when we say we're celebrating our birthdays. If we're sisters? Cousins? We don't resemble each other. My mouth is dry when he's surprised at what we do—a professor and a compliance officer. And I am fucking done when he tells us that the University of Richmond, Kaya's and my alma mater, is a *really hard* school to get into now.

Sayers, her ear trained from the deck chair, props herself up. She visits Arizona at least once a year, has family here, knows the sun's dusty-rose lumber over the mountains. She's been wondering all week if she might have to assert her whiteness in a moment like this to prompt someone else's silence.

"It was when we went, too," I murmur, as I return my craned neck to the headrest of the floater, glance at Kaya looking back at me from hers.

Somewhere behind the pool bar, someone turns on Erykah Badu.

We laugh. We know it's for us.

Ex. 3: Jackson, Mississippi (November 2023)

Being in Jackson for the fiftieth anniversary convening of the Phillis Wheatley Poetry Festival is like being at a family reunion. Except I only know a handful of people, which I guess is not unlike my actual family reunions. I am meeting poetic aunties for the first time, snuggling siblings, and connecting with cousins I only know in name. I'm here because the assistant director of the Furious Flower Poetry Center, an institution for Black poetics at James Madison University, invited me for a panel. She works with Lauren, the director, whom I met through DaMaris, when we were all at the NAACP Image Awards days before the world shuttered itself in 2020. This is the way the introductions unfold among attendees as we mapped the matrix of our connections. On paper, we are crowded in cold conference rooms and thick-aired theaters to discourse and listen to one another's work, but, in reality, we are here to feed and get fed.

Each session is a church service—a liturgy. Sometimes our preachers break into song; others offer an opportunity for a call and response. On the first full day, Airea D. Matthews delivers a poetic benediction. And even as I am surrounded by women reciting lines from Margaret Walker's "For My People," momentarily ashamed I don't know all the words to this hymnal, I am moved by the spirit—want to stretch out my arms with a praise on my lips.

But as we worship the words and the ligatures that link us together, our collective glossolalia elevating us, our presence in the space is not without encumbrance. Writer Jasmine Holmes draws our attention to this as she introduces one of the plenaries. She notes that the year of the festival's first convening was marked by the *Roe v. Wade* decision, the birth of hip-hop, and the ceasefire and removal of combat troops from Vietnam; however, now, the year we reconvene, Congress supports Israel's purported retaliation against Hamas, the Supreme Court has overturned *Roe*, and misogynoir is a pillar of hip-hop culture. Unspoken but also known: the children suffering at the borderline of our nation's humanity; the underreported crises brewing in Sudan, the Democratic Republic of the Congo, and Myanmar; and the list could go on. I press against the wall at the back of a packed auditorium, bracing myself against the way the world leans as we careen toward the 2024 election. We, as a nation, at a tipping point at which we've arrived before. And like the unraveling of Reconstruction Era policies following the Civil War that gave way to an era of segregation, we now sway the wrong direction.

In fellowship with these women, I am in a brief oasis in the desert of America. Fully hydrated, my fronds unfurl. But even in the lush fertile space we've cultivated, we see beyond its boundaries, feel the arid heat sucking up our vitality with a force that makes us conserve our resources. Over these four days, as I've bonded with women in the car for snack runs and in restaurants over oysters, I've learned that so many of us almost didn't come to Jackson. Of course, we wanted to be part of this historic gathering that celebrated women whose work paved the way for ours. Not just Phillis Wheatley, the first Black woman to publish a book in colonial America, but the women who came together in 1973 to celebrate the bicentennial of her accomplishment: Lucille Clifton, June Jordan, Audre Lorde, Sonia Sanchez, and Alice Walker. We wanted to be in communion with them as much as we wanted to be with our contemporary luminaries: Eve L. Ewing, Nikole Hannah-Jones, Imani Perry, and Jesmyn Ward.

But we are all also worn down—most of us educators shouldering the collective burdens of our students during a semester many of us remarked has been as hard as ones taught in various stages of the pandemic on Zoom, in masks, and to hybrid classrooms. And though we don't discuss it much, we wear the weight of Jaylen Burns—a Jackson State University student murdered near campus two weeks prior. And still, with the resilience for which we are famed, we turn into one another, against the world, for a few days of intellectual rigor, which is why I decide to skip a virtual department meeting for my job to listen to the Alice Walker talk.

During her plenary, Walker explains how she was working through her seminal text *In Search of Our Mothers' Gardens: Womanist Prose* when she came to the first festival. In honor of that, she has taken to the stage with Ebony Lumumba, the Jackson State University English professor responsible for the gathering. Their conversation is perhaps supposed to be geared toward the legacy of that work and Walker's spearheading of the womanist movement; however, the dialogue also moves with the spirit. Walker delivers short sermons as answers to Lumumba's questions. The room resounds with affirmation as Walker reminds us that our minds are homes we can be run out of, as she asks us how we can be happy if we're afraid to be.

I tune my ears to teenage Chet'la's frequency, who first read Walker's "Everyday Use" in high school. The short story about honoring lineage taught me the value of lived interaction with my long-gone ancestors. I recall it when I don my great-grandmother's locket or stack my Nana's gemstone eggs on my altar. While I listen to Walker, I wish my relationship with her work could be cast in amber, frozen in those times alongside my first read of *The Color Purple*. But Walker's more recent alignment with authors espousing antisemitic and transphobic rhetoric gives adult-me pause, and, as ashamed as I am to admit this, I want to divorce her work from her harm.

When I was a junior in high school, my class read Mark Twain's *The Adventures of Huckleberry Finn*. My teacher, new to teaching, wanted to preserve the integrity of the literature; he explained that he wouldn't censor the text when he read it aloud. Twain's novel uses "nigger" no fewer than two hundred times. Our teacher invited us, a room of teenagers, to make our own decisions as we popcorn-read passages. I listened to him and the mostly white classmates I'd known for three years in my school's small honors program use the word, over and over again. I don't know which was worse: listening to those for whom "nigger" fell from their tongues as if they were saying "homework"; or listening to those who took a pause, met my eyes, then dipped their chins as they uttered it. In real time, my white teacher realized his error. After class, he told me I didn't have to attend for the rest of the unit, even as he explained Twain to be demonstrating the vernacular from the time to expose its racism.

Years later, as an educator, I can follow some of my teacher's logic to invite students to understand the text for what it was. He wanted us to sit with the complicated attempt at social commentary through the use of racist language. He wanted us to cultivate a capacity for conversing about the gray—for which so few of us in our contemporary cancel culture have space. But his decision to allow students to read the word aloud is unfathomable. All it did was cause damage and harm. While for so many, Walker has been a beacon, her beliefs and words have injured.

It is hard for me to full-head nod to her with this in my mind, even though we align on a liberated Palestine. It's the way I hope it's hard for people to read Flannery O'Connor or Alice Munro, to listen to Michael Jackson. I hope people feel it on the Fourth of July—celebrating the independence of a country that systematically disenfranchises, raising a glass to a document written by an enslaver who would later rape a fourteen-year-old girl he owned, "fathering" her children. Veneration can cloak people's most inhuman parts, shroud them in glowing gossamer they don't deserve. Here, basking in the glow of Walker, my heart lights, the brilliance beams between me and the other women in the room. The glare making it easier to see only beauty.

As the conversation closes, Al Green's 1972 classic "Love and Happiness" gurgles from the speakers. Walker mentioned it during the dialogue, and someone running the soundboards plays it for us. As Green's voice and the strum of a guitar croon over us, we break into smiles. And as the beat drops, Ebony and Alice find their feet—transforming from speaker and interlocutor to aunties. And like at a family reunion, within moments, the hundreds of us packed into the ballroom leave our chairs and find formation. We are singing and swaying in sisterhood, shoulder to shoulder as we bump, then hug strangers, while we step into our collective, Electric Slide rhythm. With these Black women from across the country, under the eyes of our ancestors, we shed the pummeling realities at home and abroad, our responsibilities, for better or worse. We are in our bodies, at home with one another, grateful, as we smile and shimmy back and forth to the music of a man who, under oath, admitted to beating his wife. And like at a family reunion, for the sake of a moment of mutual merriment, so much goes unsaid, as we try to hold ourselves and our elders in our complication.

heartland (noun)

3. *poetic.* a place where love resides

Ex. 1: Indianapolis, Indiana (January 2022)

My father keeps tripping over my grandmother. Once when he walked in the door. Once when he put on his coat. And once when he rose from the couch to grab the remote. Once, he looked at her as if she were a kid sneaking cookies from the cupboard and shook his head. It wasn't until my brother tripped over her, as well, and chuckled "Grandmom," as if she'd stuck out her foot, that I suggested we move her ashes farther from the front door.

My dad has cried less since she died than he did when we put down our family dog, Pacemaker—her paw pressed against him as her chest slowly ceased movement. When Pace died, it was clear he didn't know what to do with himself—eyes leaking as he walked laps in the house. It was as though the tears surprised him.

It isn't that my dad doesn't love his mother, that they weren't close. He called her "sweetie" every time they talked on the phone—tender in the way that made the role reversal between parent and child a seamless one. He's just not often outwardly emotional. For a while, my brother and I joked about the hugs Dad would give us. He's a hugger, don't get me wrong; he's someone with whom you can cuddle up on the couch. But sometimes he's quick to drop his arms—leaving you, the other hugger, holding him. My brother and I, in turn, sometimes keep ourselves wrapped around his middle longer. We do this because we want to hold the him that he is as well as the kid we see in him.

The morning Grandmom Sebree took her last breaths, my father called me after he knew I was done with my day of doctor's appointments. She wasn't vaccinated and died from a swift battle with COVID. He thought this outcome inevitable when she lumbered through her words on the phone after Christmas; when she tested positive; when she went into the hospital, from which my father said she would not likely reemerge. She was eighty-one; she had asthma.

When we'd seen her just that past August, I was scared to get too close, didn't want to be the deliverer of COVID. I sat across the living room in two KN95 masks as the surgical one she wore slipped below her nose, as a neighbor dropped off food with a cloth one looped around her arm. When my father and I left, he hugged my grandmom—proclaiming he was grown and would do what he wanted. I followed swiftly behind him. It would be the last time either of us touched her—the pillow of her shoulder, the nestle of our cheeks to hers. As we left her apartment, I let out the type of sob I do when it's a surprise—loud and sudden, guttural. I sucked air in those audible gasps that teeter toward hyperventilation, overfilled my chest with oxygen that made the world split and tilt.

My father placed a hand on my back as he guided me to our car, where he fiddled with his phone a minute before driving off. A man of more action than discussion, his plan unfolded when we pulled up to the house of my COVID-conscious cousin. She's the one with twin toddlers and a dog the same breed as Pacemaker. I knew what he was up to. He needed to scratch behind the curves of the dog's velvet ears, and I needed to have fun with little ones. This is his modus operandi—exuding a sure calm in the face of emotion. When I stumbled over the words to tell him I was queer, he asked if I wanted him to treat this as if it were news as he splashed Frank's Red Hot onto his food.

And so, now, I'm giving him what he needs: a bit of comic relief as he and my brother trip over the metal container that holds his mother, until it's time for him to say "let's go, Sweetie"—packing her into the car and driving her back east to scatter some of her on the beach.

Ex. 2: Cleveland, Ohio (February 2023)

I want to run away with the bride. Not because I am in love with her. I mean, I love her, but not in the way that should make her groom nervous. I want to run away with her because I am standing at this altar looking at her and her soon-to-be husband, and recognizing the pending shift in what I understand to be a soul friendship—those special bonds with someone with whom you feel you can be your full self.

I met Sara in Lewisburg, Pennsylvania, when she was a college sophomore and I was a post-graduate fellow. We worked in a small basement office of a poetry center, where we became work wives—scheduling our in-office time to coincide. I am six years her senior, but even from the start, when we were both in those expansive years of our early and mid-twenties, I felt grounded by her.

Our friendship is one of gentleness and a mutual understanding of our anxieties. We both replay the conversations we've had, apologize for taking up space, while assuring the other that they are never too much. In those early, Lewisburg days, we would drink our tea and slurp our bowls of pasta during dark, long winters. We both salivated for the days of fresh, homemade strawberry shortcake as spring sun started to speckle the sidewalks. And when we knew the end of my fellowship and her graduation approached, we spent increasing amounts of time together—going to CVS for tampons, sneaking in short walks and café chats between our other commitments. We both worried that the thread between us would snap as we moved to new places and stretched our adulthoods in different directions. We agreed to schedule phone dates, even as she joked to her roommates that she never wanted to be a person who had to schedule time to talk to people she loved.

But for the seven years of our long-distance friendship, we have. Our conversations evolved from college-town woes and how much we spent on a salad for lunch to how we hated the way our pants fit and the romantic partners we were considering. We've convinced each other it was okay to leave jobs and cities that left us broke and broken. We've talked about our shared gastrointestinal struggles, our credit card debts, and our desires to grow small humans. If we know the other is traveling, we send a "I see you're at the airport; have a safe flight" message, since we share our locations. And when we can sneak in scheduled phone dates, we linger for longer than we anticipated—saying we need to go but not wanting to hang up. So, instead, we clang pots cooking dinner, pop on the toilet for a quick pee, and get dressed to head out the door to meet other people we tell ourselves we want to see. When we finally hang up, we follow up with a text message.

This habit extends beyond our calls. She once sent me a card in the mail on purple card stock, with a Post-it affixed to it that read: "Apparently, I have a hard time saying goodbye even in letters 😊." What's strange, though, is I don't remember the way we first parted at the end of our time in PA. But based on our current struggle, it must have been effusive and slow.

During the pandemic, when she left her apartment in northeastern Ohio, where she was attending graduate school, to move in with a new boyfriend in the northwestern part of the state, I started to sense the shift. The frenetic energy that vibrated between us found a new rhythm in her. When they got engaged a year later, I wasn't surprised. She'd found her person.

And now I'm standing in front of an audience of their loved

ones, my fingers making wet depressions in the paper cradled between my forefinger and thumb. She had been afraid to ask me to author a poem for their nuptials, had taken me out to brunch where he actually made the request. She quickly followed up, saying that they'd pay me, that they didn't want me to work for free, that there was space to say no if the ask was too much. In my silence, she read hesitation. But none of these I wanted or felt. Her face calmed as a smile spread across mine.

So, a few months later, I am here in this Great Lakes–cold February, clearing the fist from my throat as I begin to read the poem I named for a song they love. I mention their cats and favorite coffee shop, how they fell in love when the world turned in on itself. I mostly look at their guests and the groom, as I pace myself through the words, worried my mouth's motor will otherwise falter, stall out. Near the poem's close, I finally turn to her—draped in white and dappled in light.

Although our paths have taken different turns, as the slightly older friend, I often felt I could provide some guidance about balance transfers and ginger to reset an upset stomach. But now she's merging into a future I have not, one I respect but am unsure if I'll explore. And while I have no advice, I do have a love that ekes out of each of my pores as I look at her. I want to go in for a hug, but I am afraid we'll get trapped in one of our can't-say-goodbye moments. So, instead, I give her a head tilt and a nod before I pivot on my heel, accept her brother-in-law's arm, and descend the altar away from her.

Ex. 3: Madison, Wisconsin (August 2021)

On stools in front of a dresser mirror, Dantiel and I do our hair—her five-year-old locs and my recently shorn growth. She has lived in her new home as long as I have been on the road—just a few weeks. She moved from Florida to the Midwest to be a professor. And I packed up my place in Lewisburg and took a leave from my job for research travel. We are both still sorting ourselves in this transition. She's deciding which markets she likes, and I'm mapping where I'm headed next.

My trip to Madison is the first time we've seen each other outside of writerly spheres. Pandemic Zooms cemented our friendship after meeting a few years earlier at a writing residency. On this first visit, we do fun shit: eat oysters and sea bass, dress in jumpsuits and put on bright lipstick, sing loudly into the endurant thick of August. But I'm in town for a week, so we handle adult business, as well. We clean and unpack books, figure out how to cover the transparent windowpanes of her bathroom door. And while I've given up a permanent address for exploration, there is still a life I must keep up with: storage bills, doctor's appointments, hair maintenance. I thought of the latter before I packed my CR-V, asking a stylist to cut my uneven COVID lengths up to my chin. But now, after three weeks on the road, I need to unfurl my two-strand twists, wash my hair, salve my scalp, and retwist.

I'd planned to do this in the privacy of the hotel I booked for myself in Illinois before going to stay with my friend Molly, but Dantiel needed to do hers, too, after the move. We prepped the space; spread out a mix of shea butter, coconut, and argan oils after I untwisted my hair throughout the day. Perched beside each other, talking to each other's flipped visages, we remark on how there are few people with whom we have shared this: wet necks, towels draped, hair clipped and cordoned off in a series of sections as water wiggles down our cheeks. It's intimate. We both have saved our washday rituals for ourselves and certain loved ones for various reasons, both our natural hair journeys shaped by shame and family respectability politics. But this, our heads and arms craned to make sure the manipulated strands fall in the appropriate directions, is different. This marks a graduation in our relationship from "writer-friends" to "friend-friends," as she put it.

Yesterday, a Black woman at a coffee shop also sensed our kinship. Dantiel and I were answering emails, chitchatting, and laughing, when the woman left her table to come to ours. She said she doesn't see this type of Black-woman fellowship often, having grown up in Wisconsin. We learned she's a doula. Everyone followed each other on Insta.

Tonight, Dantiel and I talk about the gift of the stranger's comment and the baby I'd recently decided I wanted, as we dip our fingertips in jars and grease our scalps. We watch *The Chair* on Netflix, and Dantiel hopes she won't be Yaz, the sole Black woman working in the show's English department. I laugh and lament that I already am, as we talk about where we want to be in a year.

We don't know, after months of fevers and joint pain and fits of vomit, I'll be diagnosed with lupus. We don't know we'll be on the phone while she's heading home from dinner when she discovers she's lost her mom. We don't know we'll spend the next summer in Rome with our friend María, where our bonds will be tested, as the difficulty of our individual lives pulls us together and apart like the varying loops of cat's cradle yarn. We don't know I'll get a job in Wisconsin, and that in turning it down, I will mourn the loss of this potential future—the softness of our damp undoneness as she palm-rolls and I twist.

In the Gallery of Good Hurt

> Beauty is not a luxury; rather it is a way of creating possibility in the space of enclosure . . .
>
> —SAIDIYA HARTMAN

"How do you know it's good if it doesn't hurt?" I asked Nikki over a spa menu, a welcomed break from our self-directed writing retreat.

She raised a *Girl, what?* eyebrow, and we laughed as we scheduled our appointments. She opted for a Swedish massage, one with a light touch to stimulate blood flow and promote relaxation. I went with deep tissue, which provides sustained pressure to target stiff muscles, relieve chronic pain. My massage therapist rubbed her thumbs down my neck, pulled it slightly right and left. But as she kneaded my knotted fascia, I kept thinking about Nikki's valid eyebrow. To what else do I apply this "good hurt" logic?

Certainly, for a long time, love. Movies and shows etched the desirability of difficult romantic entanglements in me young: the bets of *She's All That* and *How to Lose a Guy in 10 Days*; the liars in *The Wedding Planner* and *Aladdin*; the push and pull of *Love & Basketball*; and whatever the hell was going on in *Save the Last Dance*. And though I've stopped looking for good hurt in my relationships, I still sop it up in the art I seek—crying my way through *Past Lives* and *Eternal Sunshine of the Spotless Mind* in humble appreciation. Each one transporting me to reading *The Great Gatsby* for the first time as Jay dies in sight of the glimmering green light.

"War Anthem" is my favorite piece from *Woolf Works*—a contemporary ballet based on three Virginia Woolf novels. The segment centers a shell-shocked character from Woolf's *Mrs. Dalloway*; he continues to have flashbacks about a friend who died in World War I. In the show, two danseurs who represent those characters heave and fall into each other—trading off support in graceful strain. Even when they've both found the strength to move without being braced, it's a dizzying dance. Sometimes I play the scene's six-minute song for hours. It becomes the soundtrack to grading poems, to driving bands of forest and farmland, to feeling a feeling I've been avoiding. Each time, I'm transported to the show's quiet devastation—a weight in my chest I register as beautiful. In art, I seek the echo of the breadth of human experiences, but most often our hurt—emotions we are reticent to share. In the rendering of someone else's caverns, I am both more whole and less alone in my grief, my rage, my uncertainty; it's a sensation I've sought since I was a teenager.

I wrote my college admissions essay on the disquiet of Gordon Bennett's 1992 painting *Myth of the Western Man (White Man's Burden)*. I encountered it while on a school-supported trip to Sydney, Australia, the summer before my senior year. I had fundraised for months—sold packs of M&M's and Joe Corbi's pizzas—to afford the excursion, which would also take us to

Hawaii and New Zealand. Although I had once-in-a-lifetime experiences during that summer of 2005—surfing, street luge, Zorbing—one of my most vivid memories is of the painting.

The 5.7-by-9.9-foot piece features white and blue dotwork as well as paint splatters in black, red, and yellow. Around the canvas, scattered blue patches contain white-numbered years. In the painting's center, somewhat obscured by abstractions of circles and streaks, a windblown figure braces against the elements. With one foot up, cloak afloat, he holds tight to a pole staked in the ground. Above his head, a date: 1992. At his feet: 1788.

In the late eighteenth century, the Brits planted their flag in present-day New South Wales, Australia, claiming it as a colony for the empire. As with other places to which they laid colonial waste, they weren't the first people there, just the most virulent.

The rest of the years around the figure in Bennett's painting traced some of this history: the first colony (1803); the massacres of the Wiradjuri people (1824); the establishment of a tent embassy protesting abysmal Aboriginal rights (1972). The 1992 date—the most recent and highest on the canvas—represents the national case that acknowledged how British settlers displaced the Aboriginals from their traditional homelands through colonization. Bennett painted the piece in that year, in a style that was also a response to Australian history. In 1972, the government spent $1.3 million on *Blue Poles* by Jackson Pollock, an abstract expressionist painter whose style *Myth of the Western Man* mimics. This incensed the country's fiscally conservative public. In this way, Bennett's work explores both sides of his ancestry—being of both Aboriginal and Anglo-Celtic descent.

But it was years before I knew these details. At seventeen, I was taken aback primarily by the painting's physicality—its chaos and magnitude arresting. It was an experience I didn't realize I hungered for—a craving I often satiated through books. In the real world, we ask one another, "How are you?" and we respond, "Fine," regardless of whether we are. But in worlds concocted by words, I appreciated the characters' interiorities—how they chastised their desires and overworked to prove themselves. In high school, I hadn't yet known how that interiority could be communicated through visual art. But as my friends wandered other galleries, I sat in front of Bennett's work, transforming the way I had the first time I read Toni Morrison's *The Bluest Eye*.

Years later, after I further connected with the painting by its context, I hunted for visual representations of history in my travels. Seeking similar, halting encounters, I sought renderings of my experiences as a Black woman. As someone interested in the intersection between past and present through research and art, I frequented historical institutions. But as I shuffled through them domestically and abroad, rending truth from artifact, I rarely experienced the specific emotional unfurl I had with Bennett's work.

In 2018, I visited the International Slavery Museum in Liverpool, England. The city is home to one of the most significant European ports in the transatlantic slave trade, responsible for the transportation of 1.5 million enslaved Africans. That fact, coupled with the name of the museum, set my expectations. I anticipated an establishment geared toward a worldwide audience, with the stateliness of a Smithsonian-level institution. Instead, the International Slavery Museum occupies a single floor inside Liverpool's Merseyside Maritime Museum, which houses exhibits on the *Titanic* and the *Lusitania*. This reset my expectations.

Although the museum addresses forms of modern slavery, it centers the transatlantic slave trade and its legacy. Even as I settled on that, I was disquieted by some quotes that lined the entry hall, inviting visitors into galleries. Among them, a 1912 quote from former US president Woodrow Wilson: "The history of liberty is a history of resistance." A year after stating this, Wilson, a famed racist, enforced segregation in the federal government.

After walking through renditions of West African villages and cowrie shell headdresses, I entered a Middle Passage simulation. It included a video featuring a Black person's body parts—arms, legs, torso—set to the soundtrack of their groans and the clank of moving chains. I then entered the section on slavery in the Americas; however, the presented objects that lodged in my gums like popcorn kernels were the ones not explicitly about the oppression's horror. A display of china, silverware, and finery featured labels explaining that these items represented those that enslaved people would use during their "service" on plantations. A reproduction of a painting showed a shirtless enslaved woman in the background behind an enslaver with his shirt untucked; the accompanying text did not mention the image's lascivious nature. Even the units of measurement confused me—listed in pounds and ounces, even though the metric system is the standard unit of measurement in most countries. Wasn't this museum supposed to be geared toward an international audience?

I had similar questions concerning intended audience at the National Museum of African American History and Culture in Washington, DC—the only Smithsonian institution on the National Mall that centers the African American experience.

NMAAHC was over a hundred years in the making. In 1915, Black Union Army veterans formed a committee in hopes of developing a national memorial for African American achievements. Although they had incremental success in the creation of the museum—including the opening of the federally chartered but privately funded National Afro-American Museum and Cultural Center in Wilberforce, Ohio, in 1981—NMAAHC didn't open until September 2016. People traveled by the busloads to see this new monument to our culture. Free timed-entry passes would sell out in hours after the museum released a new thirty-day batch of them. But while on a trip for a conference in February 2017, I snagged a ticket.

The celebration of Black history and contemporary culture vibrates the walls. I smiled at the history I'd known—Negro spirituals, Tommie Smith and John Carlos's Olympic fists, the legacy of Sidney Poitier. But I also learned—delighted by the stories new to me. I'd known about Black Patriots in the American Revolution, about Crispus Attucks and those who enlisted to serve in return for their freedom. But I knew not of the Bucks of America, an all-Black unit protecting merchants in Boston, or of the silken flag they were issued in honor of their service.

NMAAHC encourages guests to begin at the beginnings of African American history and move toward present day. The historical floors are in the basement, while contemporary and cultural exhibitions occupy the top three. I understand the logistics of this—entering the dark to come into the light.

But this historical progression meant that—like in Liverpool—to move forward, I had to go through the slave trade and Middle Passage—a cavernous room emulating the hull of a ship. A quote from Olaudah Equiano, who survived the "loathsomeness of the stench, and crying together," illuminates a wall. And although I didn't feel the same visceral discomfort I did at the International Slavery Museum, I did continue to feel the creeping presence of whiteness. Quotes from captain's logs and letters reminding me that those in power control the narrative, the archive.

The museum's role is to educate, to present histories that have been erased, subdued, to introduce complexity. And while I know the founding of this country is predicated on slavery, I am always struck by the Paradox of Liberty section of that first basement floor in NMAAHC. After walking through the Middle Passage, as well as colonial- and revolution-era America, visitors enter a three-story space from which they'll be able to look at a wall lined with quotes for the duration of the historical exhibits.

As we enter the slightly lighter space rendered in gray, tan, and black, the wall reads "The Founding of America" and has a quote from the Declaration of Independence: "All men are created equal . . . with certain unalienable rights . . . whenever any form of government becomes destructive of these ends, it is the right of the people to alter or abolish it." Beneath the imposing quote, a statue of its author: Thomas Jefferson. He stands atop a platform called the Paradox of Liberty, surrounded by bricks. Those prisms represent some of the over 600 people he enslaved. Some of them bear names like Sally Hemmings—spelled this way in honor of how her descendants spell their surname—and the children she had by him.

This imagery is intentionally ironic. I assume museum curators want visitors to grapple with the juxtaposition of this Founding Father looming large over objects, not people, under the language of liberty he wrote. But each of the times I've been to the museum, I'm irritated in a place I want to feel no irritation. Why does he get to take up space in a place meant for *our* historical preservation? How, even here, is he rendered looming large and human, while the Black people who labored for his happiness, to borrow Jeffersonian phrasing, are rendered disembodied from anything resembling their humanity? He believed us "inferior to whites in the endowments both of body and mind," which the Paradox of Liberty platform painfully replicates.

Why not a statue of Isaac Granger—a blacksmith enslaved at Monticello, of whom we have both photograph and recorded memoir? Granger's recollections of Jefferson being a "mighty good master" could have embodied some of that contradiction. Or, if curators were looking for someone working toward the founding of early America, why not Prince Hall—a Black abolitionist living in Boston who worked for liberation and education? Or Benjamin Banneker, who stands astride from Jefferson on the platform? Banneker—a free Black mathematician and astronomer—wrote Jefferson to call out the hypocrisy of him being both an enslaver and the father of American independence. The museum highlights this epistolic exchange; it's farther back on the platform—along with the poetry of Phillis Wheatley, whose work Jefferson dismissed. Every time I come upon the unavoidable platform presenting the paradox, I am overcome, as I was by Bennett's work in Australia. But not in a way that evokes yearning. There is no good hurt here.

In Tina Campt's *A Black Gaze: Artists Changing How We See*, she distinguishes depictions of the Black experience from the embodiment of it in art. She argues that mere renderings of Black life—of our culture and history—position it "in ways that allow it to be engaged at a safe distance or viewed at arm's length through a lens of pity, sympathy, or concern." Campt explains that this maintains the "existing limitations of traditional ways of narrating the Black experience." The representation of enslaved laborers as bricks reinforces how we were once seen, how some people still see us presently.

People go to museums to be reflected, to be connected, to understand the human condition, the natural world, the universe. It's these experiences I pursue when I stumble into a film or show that cleaves me, lances the hot, infected boil of emotional stagnation—a pus release that hurts but relieves. Expelled of bad humors, I am more present in myself—distracted less by the pain. The emotional range of our existence enlivens me—from the bruised, split lips of birth to the pungence of lily blossoms. This is why I love the dysregulated landscape of toddlers. They can simultaneously experience joy about their new toy and sadness over the windblown tree branches, something we unlearn with age. I comb through museums in search of that range—a smile and a frown colliding around each corner, reacquainting me with my childlike id, with a flood of emotions.

But in some of those historical institutions, I was not experiencing an ache that felt productive. This was in part because they presented my history for someone else, for someone for whom my suffering needed to be made real. So, in my travels, I pivoted away from those museums and toward visual art ones, which more often replicated the initial ache I'd endured. I sought what Campt calls a Black gaze: "Neither a depiction of Black folks or Black culture, it is a gaze . . . that shifts the optics of 'looking at' to a politics of *looking with, through, and alongside another.*" In art, I seek not a reproduction of what happened to us, but the echo of the breadth of human experience we sometimes fear, squander, keep hidden deep within ourselves.

I get that massage-like good hurt when I view Alison Saar's work. The Los Angeles–based visual artist centers Black women's experiences. Her art takes the shape of sculptures, prints, and mixed media. One of my favorites is *Coup* (2006), a figurative sculpture of a Black woman sitting straight-backed in a chair, clutching a pair of scissors with both hands. Behind her trails baggage bound by rope and tied to her by a long braid of her hair. Although she is tethered, she has agency in her hands. With her shears, she could sever herself from the suitcases. And yet, as a stagnant sculpture, she's forever bound. This beautiful balance, this emotional precipice, is prevalent in much of Saar's work.

Black studies scholar Christina Sharpe describes Saar's figures as "powerfully evocative, painful, and beautiful, [as] they visually and physically reference histories of race / sex / violence." She goes on to say how "these sculptures get at the varied and multiple conditions of Black women." They demonstrate how, even in our quotidian struggles, we are empowered, beautiful. Saar's works "engage the body and the spirit," Sharpe states, as they are not meant to be simply viewed, but viscerally experienced.

Saar is part of a contingent of Black women sculptors creating works that "offer a multi-perspectival vision of history that 'fills the deliberate gaps and distortions of the historical record,'" explains curator Rebecca McGrew, who quotes bell hooks. In this way, Saar's art is not just an embodiment of my experiences—far more alive than the brick representations of enslaved Africans stacked around Jefferson—but an embodiment of the *disruption* of whiteness I crave in museum spaces.

In the Victoria and Albert Museum in London, I usually breeze through the Dorothy & Michael Hintze Sculpture Galleries—a main thoroughfare on the ground floor. The V&A houses some of England's preeminent collections—home to nearly three million objects from over five millennia, including millions of representations of white people. While I appreciate Michelangelo and Rodin's work, my attention wanes as I pass through the sculptures, framed by floor-to-ceiling windows. After spending a day at a museum surrounded by marble busts and Renaissance Christian iconography, I crave a week-old Krispy Kreme more than I do the white-bodied imagery.

But in 2023, as I prepared to leave the museum after checking out the *Diva* exhibition, I stopped and saw, nestled between two marbled white women, a Black woman who looked like me—not just in bust color, but in features. There—with full lips, broad nose, and hair slicked back in a bun with laid baby hairs—stood *Lay It Down (On the Edge of Beauty)* (2018), cast in granite and bronze. Around the corner, in bright, gold-colored metal, next to marble men in a struggle, a statue of a Black man taking a selfie in sweats: *Signals* (2021). The artist, Thomas J. Price, worked with the V&A to cultivate this interruption to the sculptures of old, of Greek and Roman figures. "I want people to recognize themselves and feel valued," he explained. And I snapped shots of the figure in *Lay It Down*'s kitchen.

In the label about the presentation of these contemporary sculptures alongside historical ones, the museum explains:

> "From a young age, Price has been aware of who gets to be depicted in European art, and how that affects our vision of social value and power. He carefully selects materials, scale, and display methods to subvert sculptural traditions, addressing issues of visibility and identity."

And, in doing so, the white sculptures dominating the gallery, for me, fell from view.

But the juxtaposition of bodies and eras between Price's Black figures and the busts of white ones also amplifies the historical obfuscation. For so long, these spaces refused to figure us. These museums have featured work that painted us in the background as servants, as accoutrements, if we were present at all (aside from in the artifacts we created that imperialists pillaged). I felt a balanced weight in Price's representation: a beauty *and* an ache, but disruption is different than inclusion. A disruption, an interruption, forces those who may have never thought about the fact that we were missing to face it, to see, alongside me, what it means for the hidden to be revealed.

Campt asserts that a Black gaze "is a viewing practice and structure of witnessing that reckons with the precarious state of Black life in the twenty-first century." It "transforms this precarity into creative forms of affirmation"; it "requires both effort and exertion." Price's installation and Saar's work both do this for me. But their pieces that I've encountered are figurative—the precarity exists in looking at the Black body.

But they, and other artists, are able to arrive at this nexus of affirmation and exertion in other ways, as well.

At the Baltimore Museum of Art, I searched for Nekisha Durrett's *Frontier* (2023), a piece the museum commissioned her to create in conversation with Harriet Tubman's legacy. Durrett resisted the suggestion that she make a portrait, despite having made other figurative work. Instead of capturing Tubman's likeness, Durrett created an installation that invites us, as viewers, to step into history. *Frontier* features a black reflective panel bifurcated by a white light, which represents Tubman's propensity for prophetic visions. Durrett framed the mirrorlike surface with soil gathered from the base of the Witness Tree in Preston, Maryland—a flowering tulip poplar that likely stood when Tubman escaped enslavement nearby. *Frontier* would affirm my existence in its reflection, remind me that I, too, am art, am part of the frontier of the Black experience.

I first met Durrett at an artist residency in 2016, where we toiled by day in our studios, then gathered for sustenance in the evenings. Since then, her work has continued to punctuate my art experiences—I've been struck by her polymer clay James Baldwin rendering at the National Portrait Gallery; bathed in the multicolored light of her *Airshaft* (2021) installation in a windowed passageway at the Phillips Collection; stopped by her *Magnolia* (2021) project while doomscrolling on Instagram.

During the first spring and summer of the pandemic, Durrett started collecting fallen magnolia leaves as she wandered Rock Creek Cemetery in DC. The strolls helped her process her stress around the dual devastation of the coronavirus and police violence. In an article for what would later be an exhibit at Cody Gallery, Durrett explained her inspiration: "I mentioned how beautiful the [magnolia] tree is and she [a friend] seemed to only lament how difficult it was to get rid of the leaves . . . I started to think of these leaves as Black women." Durrett began gathering them.

Magnolia was inspired by the #sayhername movement, which responds to the lack of coverage concerning police violences against Black women, as Black men often garner media attention. Durrett punctured Black women's names into the leaves, ones whom law enforcement members murdered. Placed inside light boxes, the names of these women shine bright through the foliage—the violent context made beautiful, revealing a truth we never want repeated, even as it is. I wonder if she will continue to add names—like Sonya Massey's—to the thirty-piece project. In Durrett's work, like with Saar's, I see myself in the rejection of Black women's perpetual erasure, in the violence that exists adjacent to us.

It doesn't *not* hurt to look at *Magnolia,* to flip through the exhibition binder and read the stories of those murdered women. It's like that crick in my neck I've had since I herniated a cervical disc. The muscles around it stronger but never fully recovered. Massages help relieve the tension of remembrance from the initial injury. I may feel a little battered and bruised after, but the attention also shakes something loose. In my travels, I search for art like Durrett's and Saar's to massage me in between other museum experiences that dislocate me from myself. Back in my body through their work, I feel taller, cervical spine stretched, shoulders moving away from my neck.

But the power in viewing their work, even in the heartbreak

of the lighted names of murdered women, is that the hurt isn't primary—more of a contact high from a hot-boxed car than sucking smoke into my bronchi. In that way, the art is both an acknowledgment of my reality and a reprieve from it. Within the cool walls of a gallery, I get to choose how much I want to absorb in a curated space that can—but not always—be safe.

The Two Mississippi Museums is a state institution in the capital city that houses the Museum of Mississippi History and the Mississippi Civil Rights Museum. Linked by a foyer, the museums "take visitors through the sweep of Mississippi history and the state's role as ground zero in the US Civil Rights Movement." I went to it with the intention of feeling disruption.

I'd done this before. A year earlier, I went to the National Civil Rights Museum housed in the Lorraine Motel in Memphis, where Martin Luther King, Jr. was assassinated. My local friend Martha warned me about following the museum beyond its initial conclusion, the rooms where he stayed, across the street from the Legacy Building. The visitor experience started how I'd expected: life in western Africa; the Middle Passage; slavery and the founding of America; the Civil War; Reconstruction and Jim Crow. But at the National Civil Rights Museum, the interpretive experience delved into the mid-century movement and King's involvement. Almost imperceptibly, visitors wind a walkway upward to the second floor, where we end up in a nook carved out between two motel rooms. They replicate the ones MLK stayed in before stepping onto the balcony where he died. The rooms appear *in medias res*—or in the middle of things, in an epic sense. Museumgoers feel like flies on the wall, standing behind dressers and TV sets, looking at disheveled bedding and fake half-finished food covered by a napkin. Mahalia Jackson's "Take My Hand, Precious Lord," which she sang at King's funeral, bellowed overhead. I stood in silent reverence of the slain reverend. This could have been the end.

But against my friend's caution, I carried on to the Legacy Building. It housed the Boarding House exhibitions, which contained a replica of the place from which James Earl Ray shot the civil rights leader. The space explores the details of the assassination case: the murder, the investigation, and the conspiracy theories. But, standing there, looking at bed linens, ballistic reports, and the view of the famed balcony, I kept thinking how the National Civil Rights Museum invites guests to end their visit standing in the shoes of a murderer. The dissonance between the commemoration and the violence resonant.

I anticipated a similar dissonance between the state history section and the Civil Rights one at the Two Mississippi Museums; however, I only ended up going to the latter. I went with Dr. Joanne Gabbin—the founder and inaugural director of the Furious Flower Poetry Center, a Black poetry institute. I was honored to be joined by this literary steward, this elder. When we checked in at the information desk, a museum associate explained we were in for something special. The youngest Freedom Rider, Hezekiah Watkins, would deliver a short program.

As we entered, Dr. Gabbin and I could see him waiting in a round forum area. He reminded me of my maternal grandfather when he was young—a warm-natured man holding court in his cream, zip-neck sweater and slate slacks. My Pop-Pop Raymond was good for telling a story that ran too long but still had you buckled up for its side trips and detours. Mr. Watkins exuded the same charm. We exchanged polite hellos before the program started, and I tucked into a rounded couch with a handful of other Black women, most of them elders, too.

Mr. Watkins proceeded to tell a Pop-Pop-length tale. It started with him being a boy watching afternoon television, during which he first encountered the Freedom Riders. Enlivened by their fight for the integration of interstate public transit, he went to the Jackson bus station, where they were supposed to arrive, to catch a glimpse of them. He lied to his mom, said he wasn't feeling well, and skipped church with a friend to ride bikes downtown. While they waited and played, as thirteen-year-olds do, his friend jokingly pushed young Hezekiah into the main doors of the bus station. It was 1961 in segregated Mississippi. "Main doors," of course, meant "whites only."

Once inside the station, he found himself in the hands of a white policeman, who assumed young Hezekiah was one of the Freedom Riders that other officers missed when rounding up the protesters earlier. Law enforcement detained and jailed the revolutionaries at the request of the Mississippi State governor Ross Barnett—a segregationist who would say, "We don't want to break their bones. We only want to break their spirits." Without due process, officers sent Hezekiah to Parchman Farm, a maximum-security penitentiary over a hundred miles north. There, they assigned him to death row without explanation or cause; he was cellmates with two men convicted of murder. Sixty years later, Mr. Watkins still struggled to articulate the hunger and abuse he endured during his five-day stint in prison.

After a call from President John F. Kennedy, who inquired about minors being held at Parchman, Governor Barnett ordered Hezekiah transferred back to Jackson and released to his mother's care. Mr. Watkins recounted their joyous reunion, how his mother made him promise he would never join the Civil Rights Movement. But shortly thereafter, Freedom Rider James Bevel approached Hezekiah about joining the group. Despite initial resistance from both him and his mother, eventually he did.

By this point in the story, when he pivoted to the work he did and his subsequent arrests, the room was filled with people standing and sitting, enraptured by the conversation. As he continued, a white woman started to approach those of us seated directly before him. She lurked in my periphery. She crouched, came closer, walked all the way over. She came up to me and whispered, "Can I sit there?" She pointed to the couch. I looked to my left, where Dr. Gabbin sat, and to my right, where there was a stranger. I met the faces of the Black women around me with consternation. Puzzled, I wanted to ask: *Where?* But I knew what she wanted—me to move to accommodate her. There, in the sermonic presence of Mr. Watkins, who fought for me to be seated where I was, she wanted me to move. She didn't see the irony. Again, I felt no good in this hurt.

Jacob Lawrence's *The Migration Series* consists of sixty small, enumerated paintings on the Great Migration. Each one has a caption that maps the mass movement of Black Americans from the agrarian South to the industrial North. They outline why Black Americans left: to escape racism and injustice; to leave the farm industry's environmental decimation; to move toward the promise of better employment. The series also outlines how their arrival wasn't seamless—the crowding of trains and migrant housing, the hostility of white people everywhere.

In sixty vignettes, Lawrence's work paints an important history, but I've never seen the series together in its entirety. Half of them, all of the odd-numbered ones, live at the Phillips Collection in Washington, DC. The other half at the Museum of Modern Art in New York. Although the art itself is striking, I'm often more struck by its permanent fracture—reunited only occasionally for a special exhibition. It's emblematic for what it means for me to be a Black American: to be both bound and capable of freedom; to be both beautiful and discarded; to be dislocated at times even in my own history, my own body.

But contemporary art, historical interpretation, curation, and visitor experiences aren't exclusive entities; I know that they *can* work in concert to get at that good hurt. In June 2023, Thomas Jefferson's Monticello—the plantation of the father of American independence—opened its Contemplative Site. The memorial commemorates the lives of those he enslaved—represented as bricks in the Paradox of Liberty exhibit. The central haunt of Jefferson's 5,000 acres was the mountaintop. On it stood his home and Mulberry Row, the main street of plantation life. Positioned at the end of the vegetable garden and that significant stretch, the Contemplative Site is a new fixture of visitor engagement.

Etched into the memorial's sixty-foot-long steel wall are the names of those enslaved—revealing, on the other side of their names, the foliage of the landscape. A collaborative of architects, historians, and the descendants of those whose ancestors' labor developed the site. Historian Niya Bates shares that "descendants chose materials, set guidelines on appearance and accessibility, and were decision-makers for much of the artistic process"; that they "were as much artists as they were informants, enabling Monticello and the design team to take chances and design around major voids within the record."

The collective decided to present the names of the enslaved in chronological order. Bates describes how this "shows the evolution of enslaved communities through time, so that these names are grouped by people who would have lived and worked here together." Importantly, the site also leaves spaces for those whose stories have not yet been discovered—their presence acknowledged by absence.

Bates has worked on several Black preservation projects and strives to support contemporary artists in historically inspired creations—Sonya Clark, Ta-Nehisi Coates, Jabari Jefferson. In conversation, she shared: "I like working with people who can look beyond the archive in a way that historians can't," as "an avenue towards healing in a way that I don't think we could do if we just relied on the archive and historians." She, through her interpretive work, curates and preserves in the tradition of Campt's gaze. And I am shocked to feel cared for in a place like Monticello, through the careful cultivation of her and others' thoughtful minds.

These museums, these sites, and their complexities, exist at the limen of pain and relief. In the presence of the curation, cultivation, and creations of those who see us, I am able to be present in my full body. The galleries of good hurt remind me of a truth that lives in me even if I can't, for survival's sake, acknowledge it daily. Even though there may not be a consistent rest or relief, the release offers me what I need to head back into the world—a little more fortified and a little less alone.

Part Three

WHERE DO YOU BELONG?

American Passports

SURNAME:	Sebree
GIVEN:	Chet'la
NATIONALITY:	United States of America
BIRTHPLACE:	Chester, Pennsylvania, United States of America
ENTRY STAMP:	Munich, Germany, European Union
YEAR:	2004

I first stamped my passport a month shy of sixteen. My father and I tagged along on my mother's business trip to Munich—her first international one. This was monumental for my bootstrap parents, who had less than one hundred dollars between them when they got married in the mid-eighties; for my mother, who had my brother as a teen. When I was little, she worked as a chemist for a company that left holes in her clothes. She didn't want a life where her kids couldn't hug her until after she showered. So after years of doubt and difficulty—which included attending law school and caring for two children while my father was out at sea with the Navy—she'd fashioned herself a chemical patent attorney. The Munich trip was representative of how she'd entered her Clair Huxtable era (before we realized how complicated a *Cosby Show* reference would be).

In München, as we took to calling it, I marveled at the intricate, neo-gothic architecture of Neues Rathaus in Marienplatz. The building houses a clock that features a forty-three-bell glockenspiel and thirty-two life-sized figurines. Two to three times a day, it tells tales as the figures dance, joust, and marry. My dad and I watched it several times as we explored the city while my mom attended meetings. Each repeated performance, I took note of something new—a jousting tournament, a group of dancers—lapping it up like the sweet splendor of white asparagus soup.

We delighted in being tourists. And aside from our garbled attempts to say "*Sprechen Sie Englisch?*" when buying water, we'd committed little pre-trip German to memory. While strangers often read us as American, a few mistook us for French. I found a thrill in this, already programmed to link Eurocentrism with sophistication—the imperialization of my imagination. But each inquisitor quickly returned me to my place with disappointment on their face when they registered our country of origin.

One night, after a meal of meat, potatoes, and Riesling with one of my mother's American colleagues, the four of us squeezed into a taxi back to the hotel—us three ladies in the rear, my dad in the passenger seat. The driver, excited to chat, pointed out the places that survived the bombing of Munich in 1944, the sections that had been rebuilt. Allied Forces decimated fifty percent of the city to limit production of Nazi fighter planes in World War II. We *ooh*ed and *ahh*ed at the clash of modernity and history, the way present mirrored past in some of the reconstructions.

My mother's colleague, a white woman, leaned forward from her back seat perch—seat belt dug into her collarbone. She asked, "Who bombed the Germans, anyway?"

Not steeped in the bone-deep anxiety born in my Blackness, she asked this question in earnest. The driver pivoted his head to my father. Then, he looked back at the road.

I turned to her and said, "We did."

But who was this "we"?

We drove along silently.

SURNAME:	████
GIVEN:	Mahsa
NATIONALITY:	Iran
BIRTHPLACE:	Tehran, Iran
ENTRY STAMP:	Middletown, Delaware, United States of America
YEAR:	2002

Mahsa, Shavana, and I sat in a row in our high school honors classes; our last names followed one another's in the alphabet. This was how we became friends, often clustered together for small group assignments. We were all new to the school in 2002, and we were some of the few people of color in those classrooms—Persian, Guyanese, and Black, respectively. But even when classmates called us the Model UN, we rarely discussed race. The only time it regularly came up was during standardized test season. Shavana and Mahsa would ask proctors which bubbles to fill in under race/ethnicity. The usual answer: "Asian," until senior year when Mahsa was prompted to fill in "White/Caucasian." We joked about this, then moved on. We had teen stuff to focus on: Dairy Queen or Taco Bell for lunch; the merits of Sean Patrick Thomas over Elijah Wood. But it wasn't as though racism wasn't on the menu. Our favorite teacher junior year (ironically, no sarcasm here) "affectionately" called us "The Jim Crow Row." This was the same class where he let students say "nigger" when we read aloud *Huck Finn*. We noted these infractions, then carried on.

More often, the overt displays of patriotism were the ones we were aggrieved by—rolling our eyes at "God Bless the USA" playing from a flag-flying pickup truck. Those years, Shavana and I refused to say the Pledge of Allegiance. I'd grown up in a Quaker school where we didn't have that homeroom practice, and Shavana was a baby anarchist. We couldn't understand why people were so passionate about this America—or *'Merica*, which we mocked, said with our chins tucked and an upward nod. We were against it. We wouldn't have used these words then, but in retrospect, we were critiquing the intersection of whiteness and nationalism that was foreign to us, especially Mahsa, who was only two years into her asylum.

Mahsa's family emigrated from Tehran in 2000. They left because of religious persecution as Bahá'ís living in an Islamic State. Mahsa had to hide who she was in order to be educated—her brother already having been kicked out for their faith. Bahá'ís in Iran are routinely denied jobs, detained, imprisoned. When she was twelve, her parents told her to pack for a trip to Austria; they pulled her from class, told her to bid farewell to her friends. Mahsa did not know they would not return to Iran. In Vienna, they waited for six months to be granted passage to the United States.

Two years later, when we were freshman, Mahsa had learned idioms like "popping a cherry," but she had not yet learned about segregation. "Jim Crow Row" meant nothing to her when we were juniors—our US history course focused on America's participation in the World Wars. But she knew sometimes classmates "jokingly" called her "the terrorist," that she wasn't yet a US citizen—that surety wouldn't come for another five years. So on those high school mornings freshman year, when Shavana and I stood with our arms hung low and mouths closed, exercising our First Amendment rights, Mahsa placed her hand over her heart and pledged allegiance to this new nation and its god. It was the year after 9/11.

SURNAME:	██████████
GIVEN:	Shavana
NATIONALITY:	United States of America
BIRTHPLACE:	New York, New York, United States of America
ENTRY STAMP:	Sydney, New South Wales, Australia
YEAR:	2005

The summer after our junior year, Shavana, Mahsa, and I traveled together to Australia, Hawaii, and New Zealand on an educational trip with a dozen or so other rising high school seniors. In Australia, we journeyed from Sydney to Brisbane in a motor coach that cruised the coast. We wandered galleries and learned to surf the chop of winter waves in the South Pacific Ocean. We held koalas that smelled of piss and ate sandwiches on small-town streets.

We all loved K'gari—which still went by its colonized name, Fraser Island, then. The UNESCO World Heritage Site, ancestral home of the Butchulla people, is the largest sand island in the world. We learned about red gum, swamp box, and cypress pine, and drew our names in coastline. At night, our guide, Shannon, explained to us the sky as the Southern Cross unveiled her slight figure. At seventeen, it hadn't occurred to my me-centric self that the celestial canvas would be painted differently in the southern hemisphere. Feet deep in sand under foreign stars, I wondered what Mahsa's desert nights looked like in Iran.

My journals now remind me of what remains unforgettable: the food poisoning in Sydney; the soft-porn programming we flipped through to Mahsa's horror; the Ibis not having washcloths. I loved the drive through the Blue Mountains, where we learned their name came from the color expressed when the eucalyptus oils meet UV rays. On the coach, eyes glued to the window, Shavana mused whether Australians search for eagles in America the way we look for kangaroos here.

Going into the trip, I expected it to be less disorienting than Germany; Australians spoke the same language, at least. But like the shifted night sky, which cast Orion unfamiliar on the horizon, "barbies" and "bathers" were words I knew but had to reorient myself to. The same with "Black." I used it to identify me, but Shannon, of Aboriginal descent, explained it meant different things to different people in different places.

A guide in more ways than one, Shannon offered gentle nudges: try this, eat that, don't forget to look right. The only time he was curt was early in our week together. As we were getting our sea legs in Sydney from the hours-long journey from Hawaii, he silenced our laughter, told us not to speak while we walked through a park. I couldn't remember why he did but remember holding my breath. Like a child hiding behind their hands, I tried to make myself nonexistent. Years later, Shavana filled the gaps of my memory, explained that he shushed us as we circumnavigated an anti-Bush protest. "There was a lady with a megaphone mad about imperialism," Shavana recalled.

Australian Prime Minister John Howard had been in DC on 9/11. In line with a treaty between AU and the US, ensuring mutual investment in each other's national security, Howard backed the United States in its response to the attacks. And although Australia had initially followed America into the War on Terror, some citizens, like those back home, were tired of it and Bush's policies. In 2003, the US planned to invade Iraq to eradicate its supposed "weapons of mass destruction." Protests erupted around the world, including in Australia, where two men took to the top of Sydney's famed Opera House to paint "No War" in red. The international anti-Bush sentiment continued through his second term, bolstered by a 2005 presidential commission report that discerned there was no credible pre-war intelligence that Iraq housed these supposed weapons.

Shavana doesn't remember the specifics of the anti-Bush, anti-imperialist protest but that it was, at its core, pointing a finger at America. She *does* remember, however, that as our group cut a path away from the political gathering, we kept quiet in the face of our country's international imprint. Where we'd previously felt comfortable in our relative language skills, we felt targeted by our intonations and turns of phrase, suddenly aware of our propensity to look left when crossing an intersection. Shavana explained "I'd never felt so American" of her first-generation-ness—her mother born in Guyana, her older brother in Suriname, her elders in India.

In January 2025, following an executive order meant to "clarify" the Fourteenth Amendment, she gathered her vital documents in case there was a challenge to her birthright citizenship.

SURNAME:	Sebree
GIVEN:	Chet'la
NATIONALITY:	United States of America
BIRTHPLACE:	Chester, Pennsylvania, United States of America
ENTRY STAMP:	Ravenna, Italy, European Union
YEAR:	2008

When the light started to wane, I gathered under a wide umbrella in a Ravenna piazza with my travel companions. We were what you'd expect from a group of twenty-year-old college students, not yet legal to drink in the United States—raucous in our evening wind-downs. We donned our adult selves, sipping aperitivos and discussing our days, as we spent six weeks in Italy completing our university's language requirement.

The weekdays were routine. I'd wake on a quiet street away from the town's center where I'd have breakfast with my host mom before biking to school. I'd spend most mornings and the occasional afternoon in language class, conjugating verbs and stumbling through conversations. On those two-part days, I'd feast at wine bars on pesto, tomatoes, and penne. Other afternoons were spent at the beach—the Italian landscape an extension of the classroom.

On weekends, which started on Thursdays, we traveled elsewhere in the country. The highlights: lunch and wine, bike rides, and the (frightening to my flatland sensibilities) hike in the Dolomites. The lowlights: positioning a dresser in front of a door in a hostel in Florence; that sharp, specific pang of overdrafting my bank account again.

But by the second half of the trip, I was answering my phone "pronto" and using the correct conditional conjugation to order a cappuccino like an Italian, which meant only before eleven A.M. By then, I could read most of an Italian tourism pamphlet on Dante Alighieri, a renowned medieval poet, who died and was buried in Ravenna. In my journal, I clocked that even the not-so-great moments were a gift. I studied abroad to learn a language for which I might never have a practical use. Some might call this millennial frivolity. Others, privilege. Both would be valid. But the years my mom spent hunched in the low light of a law library were, in part, for me to enjoy this luxury.

And it, indeed, was luxurious—train-hopping through Tuscany, spooling spaghetti slick with sauce, navigating the maze of Venetian canals and getting lost. But when I sort through photos of me against a series of multi-colored buildings—tan and taupe, pale pink, faint yellow—I see the tight pull of my lips, the furrow in my brow. In the pictures, my hands grip crumpled water bottles, my hair swells with humidity. I'm dressed in odd outfits: the blue patterned halter; the gray vest; the dark, thick-fabric pants. In retrospect, I wonder who I cosplayed each day. I was astride from myself in Italy. Both there and not, in a sort of sunken place from the height of my anxieties; the soundtrack to some days as unintelligible as the adults in the *Peanuts* world of Charlie Brown.

I was a Black scholarship student on a trip with white kids whose parents paid our $60,000 tuition out of pocket. Italy amplified the distance between our circumstances. One of my classmates used his father's Amex to pay for our fourteen-person, three-course dinner one evening under black-strung bulbs and Roman starlight. I knew then that I didn't fit in—not with my mostly white classmates, and certainly not with the

Italians. I tried to quell this concern with wine that often left me stomach-sick and exhausted, as the photos reminded me. Still, I loved those nights, when the booze lowered the volume on my inner critic, when we were all just language-learning twenty-year-olds.

During one of our piazza sits, an Italian man leaned over at my end of the table. Backlit by sun pitched low on the horizon, he asked something like "*Sei uno degli americani?*" I squinted at him; tilted my head.

He thought I didn't understand, so he posed it again.

"Are you one of the Americans?"

SURNAME:	
GIVEN:	Fabienne
NATIONALITY:	United States of America
BIRTHPLACE:	London, England, United Kingdom
ENTRY STAMP:	London, England, United Kingdom
YEAR:	2023

Fabienne and I sat close at a speakeasy in Soho. We hadn't seen each other since she moved to London the year before the world went into lockdown. But we were glad to reconnect—both full of glee at the post-pandemic levels of travel and human intimacy. With the clink of our glasses, we launched into the friendship we had in our late teens and early twenties—talking of the messes we'd found ourselves in and our careers. Two self-possessed, single women, we laughed about how we'd both tried and failed to solo-haul pieces of furniture up flights of stairs: me, a mattress; her, a couch. We were still, in many ways, iterations of our old selves, the young women we were in college: her keen fashion sense, my obsession with words. We fell into an easy rhythm.

Fabienne was born in London to Ghanaian parents in the late eighties. Shortly thereafter, they moved to the United States, where she lived in Northern Virginia for her formative years. Our timelines merged when we both studied at the University of Richmond for college: me for English, her for business. We even went abroad together for a semester at the University of Warwick in England, before returning stateside to finish our degrees, after which we both moved to DC. But beyond our stint in the nation's capital, our paths diverged when she went to business school in New York, where she would study abroad in England again, that time in London.

I've long admired Fabienne's ability to flit between worlds. She's always had a sophisticated flair, even in college, with her high-necked minidresses and effortlessly styled sweats. When we studied abroad, England seemed to fit her like a good pair of black jeans. So I wasn't surprised when she studied abroad in the UK again or when she moved there in our thirties.

Over Indian food, after drinks, I asked her where she feels she most belongs. "I always felt African," Fabienne said of living stateside, never American. And I got it. My mind montaged the ways I contributed to this: my unfamiliarity with the spices she used to season her stews; my perplexity at some of her father's phrasings. Was it the *mobile*, the *lift*, the *telly*? Her response to my crinkled brow: "Queen's English." We laughed about it then, back in 2010.

But it was 2023. The Queen was dead, and Fabienne hadn't lived in the US for four years. I'd assumed in England she'd found the groundedness for which I searched, different than the unstable footing she found in Virginia. I'd guessed that, in a Radiohead sense, living in the UK made her feel that everything was in its right place. But instead, she said, she started to feel American—distinct from Black Brits. And before I could leap to misinterpret, she said, "It's like I finally have the permission to be."

SURNAME:	Sebree
GIVEN:	Chet'la
NATIONALITY:	United States of America
BIRTHPLACE:	Chester, Pennsylvania, United States of America
ENTRY STAMP:	Ravenna, Italy, European Union
YEAR:	2023

On a return trip to Ravenna, I visited Dante Alighieri's tomb.

The renowned Florentine poet was born around 1265. At the turn of the fourteenth century, for reasons too tedious to explore here but that have more to do with politics than poetry, he was banished from Florence, condemned to two years in exile, and fined. Unconvinced he'd committed the crimes for which he was sentenced, he refused to return to his hometown under anything other than honorable circumstances. Dante died shortly after finishing *The Divine Comedy*; he's widely known for its section *Inferno*—Italian for "hell." He never returned to the city of his birth, even after he left this earth—his body entombed in Ravenna.

His friend Bernardo Canaccio wrote a poem inscribed in Latin on his sepulcher. The last line reads, depending on the translation:

". . . here I lie interred, Dante, an exile from my homeland, he who was born of Florence, an unloving mother"

OR

". . . here I am enclosed, me, exiled from the earthly land, which generated Florence, mother of little love"

The sentiment of them the same.

I'd visited the tomb fifteen years before, but the memory muted. I did not recall the inscription, but I'm sure the pamphlet I'd translated in 2008 must have made mention of it. In a similar way, I cannot remember what I said to the man who asked me if I was one of the Americans—startled by his question.

I'd always wanted to divorce myself from my Americanness when I'd travel abroad, to take off the cloak of it that clung to me. When I walked into a store and parted my lips only to be confronted by an accented version of my mother tongue in the mouth of a shopkeeper, I'd decide maybe the giveaway was in my mode of dress. I'd switch my sneakers for leather sandals. This was how I've always attempted to disappear abroad, something I learned in America—wearing a rain jacket instead of carrying an umbrella in Seattle. Growing up in predominately white spaces made me hyper-visible, so I learned well how to crawl into myself, make myself small to feel safe, palatable. I straightened my hair, learned to code-switch, developed a taste for a wide range of music. I book-buried my nose on the "Jim Crow Row" the same way I stayed silent weaving through the Australian protest.

This is not something I've loved about myself.

But dematerializing the fundamental matter of me in service of others is not something I've continued wanting. I spent my twenties deprogramming. And in the same way I've never *not* been Black, in the American sense of the term, I've also never *not* been American. In the States, my Americanness comes with qualification. But each time I'm abroad, my thirst, my accent, my choices over which white countries I've stamped onto my blue passport, make me a prefix-less American.

But *I* have never been able to divorce my Blackness from my American citizenship. Perhaps that's the reality for all of us who live at an intersection of identity, for those for whom the word we add before "American" is not invisible, is perhaps the one that means more. For those of us who weren't part of the patriots' imaginations when they declared "all men are created equal."

Walking away from Dante's tomb, I paused.

Oh, America, I thought. *Mother of little love.*

Le Jardin des Arts

I stood at the window of a rented villa in the south of France as night fell—glow of the sun slipped just below the horizon, sky bright with pinholes of light.

I'd spent a jet-lagged weekend in Paris with friends before we caught an early morning train from Gare de Lyon to Nice. Our dawn-tired giggles turned to neck-breaking nods as we trundled through the changing landscape. After we left the misted morning of the City of Light, we greeted olive trees, the sea, and the sky's stormy glory in Saint Paul de Vence—the town where James Baldwin lived for the last seventeen years of his life.

For a long time, I—like I assume many Black writers in generations following him—wanted to grow up to be Baldwin. While pursing my MFA in my early twenties, I first read *Giovanni's Room,* which I started again as soon as I finished. I fell for Baldwin's clean-as-bone sentences, as he'd describe them. His language at the nexus of deceptively simple and expansive. I tore through the slim volume about two lovers in Paris in the 1940s with ease. Passages on Eden hooked me early:

> "[P]erhaps, life only offers the choice of remembering the garden or forgetting it. Either, or: it takes strength to remember, it takes another kind of strength to forget..."

From there, I inhaled the long nights Baldwin painted. The struggles real for his protagonist David, who tries to make sense of himself and his sexuality. David thought he'd find answers when he left the US for Paris, but the "questions of desire and what constitutes a home follow David across the sea," writes critic Hilton Als. In Baldwin's leading man, I saw my reflection: full of desire and longing; unclear about who I was and consumed with anxiety about it. My performance of normalcy at twenty-three in a perpetual state of precarity. David and I were both holding ourselves like fistfuls of marbles—worried a sphere might slip through our fingers, reveal a truth we weren't prepared to view.

In *Giovanni's Room,* I admired Baldwin's capacity to reach across race, time, and gender; I wanted to be involved in that type of creation.

For much of my life, all I've wanted was to be a writer. The interest scrawled in a red, spiral-bound notebook from second grade. By eleventh, I was completing a short-story collection about the most ill-fated group of adolescents you have ever met. But I wasn't always sure a writing life was possible, believed it might be just a childhood dream. Once I realized it could be more than a hobby, sometime around those first years reading Baldwin in grad school, I was fixated—an archer, pointing every arrow in my quiver at that target. As other people in my orbit amassed lives outside of work with houses, vacations, and children, the gravity of the words pulled me deeper into them. I chose to weather an ice storm at a residency in upstate New York instead of attending a friend's baby shower; participated in a three-week program instead of going to another's wedding; passed up a full-time job for a one-month opportunity to do book research.

I was living, I felt, in the spirit of Baldwin.

I wasn't just drawn to Baldwin's commitment to language; I also admired his writing life. He lived mostly overseas after his mid-twenties—spending stints in Turkey, France, and Switzerland. And even when he lived in cities like Paris and Istanbul, he often squirreled away to quieter towns to work. In an alpine village—where he lived in a chalet with his painter partner, Lucien Happersberger—Baldwin finished *Go Tell It on the Mountain*. Despite Switzerland's whiteness and its distance from the world Baldwin wrote about, it provided fertile ground from which Baldwin's work sprouted. Away from urban bustle, Baldwin could hear himself.

In part, Baldwin's life in letters took him abroad because he felt the racial stress of the US made his work, his life, unsustainable. In *No Name in the Street*, he wrote, "In America, I was free only in battle, never free to rest. And he who finds no way to rest cannot long survive the battle." He found needed recovery in France, first moving to Paris from Harlem in 1948, where he lived for nearly a decade. He then floated between European countries and the US until he moved to the south of France in 1971 after a bout of depression.

Despite his literary success, the politically fraught sixties left him bereft. He'd known Medgar Evers, Malcolm X, and Martin Luther King, Jr. Losing those men, who were fundamental to the Civil Rights Movement, within the span of five years left Baldwin not only distraught but paranoid—on the FBI's watch list for his politics and sexuality. The writing stalled, as did some of his resolve. After he had a series of breakdowns, friends in Paris convinced him to go to southern France to convalesce.

What started for Baldwin as a trip to recuperate turned into an indefinite stay in the tiny loop of a town called Saint Paul de Vence—a medieval commune on the French Riviera, its ramparts set high on green hillside overlooking the stretch of the Mediterranean called Côte d'Azur. There, a driver, a cook, and a personal secretary tended to him. There, he hosted Miles Davis and Josephine Baker, Toni Morrison and Henry Louis Gates, Jr. There, he went to the jazz festival in Nice and for dinners at La Colombe d'Or, where he befriended the owners and their children. There, he rested. And that reset allowed him to write well into the night and early morning, waking late for lunch before starting over again. Saint Paul de Vence: his own little paradise.

In October 2022, I, too, felt the paradisical gleam of southern France—its shoulder season still balmy and busy with tourists. Over the course of a week, I consumed a dozen bottles of wine with my travel mates in view of the Mediterranean and the mountains, at the intersection of coastal and alpine air. I was there to write, to follow in the footsteps of Baldwin with the support of research funding. A few friends tagged along. The experience—from the wood spoons used to ladle hand cream into my palms to the boules pit featuring a bocce team in matching wide-brimmed hats—felt like the fine filaments of a daydream. It was a life astride from the one I temporarily left stateside, where I was a professor and director in rural Pennsylvania. I had assignments to grade, contracts to renew, committee documents to peruse. But there, in France, I was a writer.

In Saint Paul de Vence, I spent most of those warm fall days sweating through my cotton button-downs and wishing I'd packed bug spray. Yet even with my bite-welted skin and wet shirts, I focused on the feel of the blue-gray cobbles beneath my footfalls, the glimmer of the Côte d'Azur. I scrawled notes in a tiny notebook on the beach, at lunch. The first night falling asleep under Baldwin's Provençal, star-cloaked sky, I thought, *What a dream.*

And it was.

But it also wasn't.

I'd been trying to get to the south of France for a while. In 2018, I applied to the La Maison Baldwin Writer-in-Residence program, which offered monthlong fellowships in Saint Paul de Vence. The organizers initially fought to preserve Baldwin's house, which had fallen into disrepair after relative vacancy for years. In 2017, the organizers lost the house-saving battle with developers, who turned the property into luxury condos sardonically called Le Jardin des Arts. Although the La Maison organizers failed to save the structure of Baldwin's home, they were committed to the preservation of Baldwin's legacy. So they created a writing residency for Black writers writing in the spirit of him. I was selected as one of them.

Although I was slated to go to Saint Paul de Vence in 2018, I was broke, living with my parents, and working four freelance jobs. Between self-employment tax, health insurance, and medical bills, most of the money that came in was already allocated. A jaunt to Europe for a month, which would mean putting off paid gigs while paying for an international plane ticket, wasn't in the budget. I deferred for a year and then deferred some more, because my money situation did not change until I got my first full-time teaching job. With a sigh of financial relief, I planned to fly to France in June 2020. Obviously, I didn't go, as the world lingered in lockdown, as bodies were stored in crowded morgues.

That summer, while trying to write in my attic office, I thought near constantly about Baldwin, especially after George Floyd's murder. I felt stupid, selfish, for wanting to be abroad, for having the audacity to want to prioritize words. My inner monologue hummed like summer night cicadas—a racket so loud, I couldn't hear myself beyond a litany of questions:

Why does writing matter when people can't breathe or find PPE? While parents are separated from their babies?

Did Baldwin feel the same?

Wasn't he sitting poolside working on the screenplay of The Autobiography of Malcolm X *when he learned of MLK's murder?*

At least his writing had meaning. What the hell am I even writing?

He deserved to be away, to escape, to find clarity.

But even when Baldwin lived abroad, he escaped nothing.

***

Despite my mind's jumble during that pandemic year before the vaccine, I was perhaps my healthiest self—on a schedule for the first time in a few years that included exercise, regular meals, and cordoned-off hours for relaxation. My hair and nails, which had started to thin, grew thick. And the loud, singular hiccups that vise-gripped my chest several times a day for two decades stopped suddenly. I rode my stationary bike in the morning and did candlelit stretching at night. On my pandemic-purchased West Elm bed, I recalibrated my relationship to rest by powering down my phone and reading each night. After a few months, I began to hear myself, as I imagine Baldwin did in the quiet caverns of his Saint Paul de Vence house. And as the cicadas dissipated, I spent long days throwing words down on the page, hoping they would amount to something.

The strain of a writing day can be hard to describe. Sometimes I send family and friends missives from places I've absconded to work: frost-gripped mountains and aqua-stretched bays. They respond: "Have fun!" I grimace but know this is partly my fault. They see sauvignon blanc and salmon at the end of the workday and read: vacation. But I send those photos because I believe my loved ones will prefer them to ones of stacks of blue-inked pages. The sunset from my desk more beautiful than the pain meds, posture correctors, and Icy Hot patches—the aids I need to get through a writing day. I don't know how to transpose how the words get stuck like an impacted bowel—strain and discomfort lasting for hours.

But there's an episode of *The Bear*—a show about chefs trying to rebuild a restaurant—that epitomizes my creative experience. In "Sundae," one of the lead characters, Sydney, attempts to develop a signature dish. A key ingredient? Submerging her palate. Mushroom adobo and mango tarts; fresh slices of pizza and caviar. Steaming bowls of soup and buns; enchiladas and short-rib hummus. While eating dumplings and pierogies, Sydney visualizes a stuffed pasta dish. Her mind cycles through shapes, sauces, and plates, as she journals and wanders through Chicago—its architecture another catalyst. Possible mock-ups appear throughout the episode in various states of arrangement: from a ring of ravioli, each topped with its own truffle shaving and basil leaf, to a Pollock-like slop of pine nuts, reduction, and spinach leaves. Finally, the imaginary dish emerges: tortellini with an aesthetic splatter of sauce comes into focus. In the final scene, Sydney preps and plates what she envisioned. She takes a bite, spits it into a napkin, and drops her head to the counter.

This is a writing day.

But despite her frustration, I am convinced that even the failure taught her something—as the twenty to thirty drafts of this essay did for me.

When I started it, I thought I was writing about Baldwin.

There's a part of me that loves to be able to hop on a red-eye on a Friday to see a sixty-year-old ballerina perform in London. To fly to Flagstaff, an International Dark Sky City, midweek to look through telescopes at the Lowell Observatory. To drive to Betterton Beach at the mouth of the Sassafras River to float with a historian, all because each feed my writing. This is a version of a life I never thought I could live as a kid, and I love it. Sometimes I look in the mirror and say: *You fucking did it, bitch.*

But like Saint Paul de Vence, this is the dream, and it is also not.

People flitted in and out of Baldwin's south of France residence—coming for a weekend and staying a month. He housed and fed them despite his money problems, entertained them over dinner into the wee hours.

The Smithsonian's National Museum of African American History and Culture has a set of photos from his time there, where he sits table-side under a tightly thatched pergola with visitors. The brilliance of his canary sweater is somewhat muted by the age of the images, but his energy pulses through. In one, his mouth is open, and his palm hovers above the table—where several forks are politely turned tines down, indicating the end of the meal. Light dapples his back and guests' faces—engaged in conversation, even as one bends to light a cigarette.

I imagine Baldwin excuses himself from his Welcome Table, as he called it, where his cook Valerie Sordello serves a *soupe au pistou* that James Beard Award–winning author Jessica B. Harris will remember forty years later. I imagine him saying: "No! Stay; drink!" with great gesticulation to the empty wine and whiskey bottles, as he tears himself away from his well-lubricated guests. He'd then retreat to the cavern of his office, cut on a lamp, and sigh into the page. He'd hear the chatter of guests outside and recall the glass-and-metal-tinned noise of writing in Paris's Café de Flore.

But I wonder, when he retreated, if this was the only life, for himself, he envisioned.

***

After a year and a half in my pandemic cocoon, I was hesitant to exit. But like a butterfly in the desert, once I emerged, my wet wings quickly dried. I fluttered, then flew. By August 2021, I was back to the frenetic flap that marked my writing career—flitting from here to there. I'd missed it, but I also hadn't. In my own cavern, I'd gained an awareness of what I'd been avoiding while living life in suitcases.

A part of me wants the steadiness of a "typical" life. Everything from my childhood, from TV to my community, tells me I am supposed to want a two-parent, two-income household with two kids, a lawn, a fence, and a dog. In that life, everyone comes home at their respective but assigned times each night. We do homework before dinner, dinner before *Jeopardy!*, *Jeopardy!* before showering, brushing teeth, going to bed. We'd start it all over again the next day. A rhythm like Baldwin's, but different. I've always been skeptical of wanting this familiar, familial routine, worried that my "desire" manifested mostly from conditioning, a desire to replicate the heteronormative models I'd seen.

But at my slowed, pandemic pace, I began to understand some of my skepticism about domesticity as a defense mechanism, that maybe I was afraid to want it. Despite my parents' divorce, I've wondered if anyone will ever love them the way they loved each other, for better and worse, for thirty-five years. More acutely, I wondered if anyone could ever love me that enduringly?

But it wasn't just my parents' marriage in my purview. In my mid-thirties, I'd started witnessing friends reorient their relationships to people they'd loved for half of their lives. I'd seen others try for months and years for babies who wouldn't come. And then others for whom a child would not arrive earthside or would and die. It was also that when I daydreamed about my future family, it was so unlike the ones I'd been presented, the ones I thought my parents would have easily accepted. I was terrified to want something so fragile, something that could break me, something that would fling me further afield from my relatives so steeped in heteronormativity and its iterations of family. But my loved ones, my true family, took my news—of my desire to have a donor-conceived child and who I was attracted to—with a quick pause and effusive love, so my concerns were mostly my mind's anxious machinations.

Sure, I could write in a murder movie–type house in winter in an empty coastal town, but falling in love and being my full self both felt tenuous. Words, I could trust. But other people? The uncertainty of human intimacy? The desire to have children? I told myself I ceased risking ruin when I stopped launching myself off swing sets twenty years ago.

For most of my life, I said I didn't want to be a parent, which might come as a shock if you, reader, have been reading these essays in order. While I've spent the past five years preoccupied with becoming a mother, for a long time I thought I wanted the inverse: forever auntie status.

It wasn't because I didn't love tiny humans. I am the first to get down on the floor to play with toy cars or scoop up a little one mid-tantrum. But in my teens, I told myself I didn't want them to mess with my body. This would come after testing unrelated to my fertility deemed I was at high risk for having children with heart issues; I figured I'd pass on the whole procreation business. Then, when I was in my twenties, kids seemed like too much responsibility, especially when I was dating a white man with a drinking problem. He wanted three to five of them and a dog, and I could never fathom how I would keep all seven of them alive. And then, the clearer I saw the stock I was from, I didn't want the weight of passing on more intergenerational trauma. But during the glacial lockdown days, the desire to be a mother struck like my libido during ovulation. And I could no longer evade the truth: I'd always wanted to be a parent.

In virtual therapy throughout the pandemic, I unspooled my resistance to motherhood, acknowledged I first felt the flare of interest a decade earlier, when I'd held my newborn nephew. I never thought I'd be an aunt. My brother lost his first love, who'd died at twenty-five, and I didn't believe he'd ever love anyone else. But when he and my now-sister-in-law brought my nephew into the world, that tiny human represented a kind of healing. As I first brought his head to my chest, I thought *I want one of these* but quickly dismissed the sentiment.

Dismissal, however, doesn't negate a thing's existence. So while I said I didn't want to be a mom, parenthood pervaded my inner life as I imagined delivery and holding a baby; childhood extracurriculars and graduation. And once I was able to hold that truth in the light, I couldn't unsee its clear imagery—a sunspot imprinted permanently.

But this epiphany illuminated other parts of my life—single ten years, living in isolated places, prioritizing work and my wants. I'd only cultivated a life that arced toward art.

While in Saint Paul de Vence with friends, I tried my hand at a Baldwin-style Welcome Table dinner. We didn't have a cook, but I wanted to play host to thank the women who'd traveled with me. They chomped charcuterie while I roasted broccoli, stirred risotto, and seared garlic-sage chicken. We sat for dinner, and I imagined myself in my own canary yellow sweater—if it hadn't been so hot. I propped my elbow on the table, fork in hand, and launched into questions about home and belonging.

Baldwin's Welcome Table dinners weren't all conversation about politics or the latest friendly gossip. Sometimes they were as much work as the time Baldwin spent at his typewriter. From the Eden-esque life he'd curated, he wasn't writing about the decadent butterfat content or lung-filling viridian. No—his eyes were trained far from the nearby two-toned water, fixated on land across the ocean. Baldwin wrote about what haunted him. The Eden that never was, the Eden that could perhaps never be: America. In his final years in Saint Paul de Vence, Baldwin spent wine-rich nights working on a memoir about his relationships with slain civil rights leaders—giving longer lives to men who never lived to see their forties.

Hilton Als writes that Baldwin's career unraveled a bit in those years, that he felt insecure about his writing. Als believes that with the publication of *The Fire Next Time,* Baldwin "had become the official voice of black America, and almost immediately his voice as a writer was compromised." Not only was his writing regarded as less "of the moment," but he, too, felt himself floundering. So sometimes his dinners would (d)evolve into a workshop space. He would read over an in-progress piece and seek constructive criticism from his guests before returning to his desk. Perhaps he turned to the Welcome Table to regulate as he wrote about the devastation of losing Medgar, Martin, and Malcolm. Or perhaps it was, as Als suggests—that the pressure of being the voice of a generation threatened implosion. He also argues that "[b]y 1968, Baldwin was finding impersonating a Black writer more seductive than being an artist."

***

At a writing conference, a mid-career poet told me she never wanted me to get famous. Whenever I relay this, friends twist up their faces. But I heard what she said in the spirit I think it was intended. I worked in literary arts administration for several years with former and forthcoming US poet laureates, Guggenheim fellows, people who would go on to win MacArthur awards. In that time, I learned so much about who I wanted to be as a creative professional. I say "professional" because a writing life involves so much more than reading, writing, and editing. There's the public self. That self gives readings and answers inquiries. It attends a series of meals where people ask the questions they didn't want to project into a microphone. (Read: inappropriate here.) Being a public self takes you away from the words and into the throes of both community and capitalism, where you make human connections with people who paid to read your work. When I worked in arts administration, I witnessed the tax artists' creativity paid, as they were away from their regular lives for days.

I also saw the toll the public self took on their personal relationships—sharing news of their impending divorce, how they took their child to a Broadway show to apologize for not being home more. Baldwin biographer David Leeming said that Baldwin's "public life as a prophet and artist made a successful private life close to impossible."

In the alpine foothills, I answered emails about the center I directed, finished a report, gave feedback on students' poems, scheduled a reading and an additional research trip. I daydreamed about a true south of France convalescence away from it all, careening boldly down the winding road to the ocean and back up to the walled city for lunch. I could so easily see myself, here, becoming the Baldwin-type I always thought I wanted to be. I wouldn't do it on the French Riviera. No—I'd go to Italy, where I had more language facilities. But I could be someone who held late-night parties, who wrote into dawn, who had people take care of me and invariably took care of no one else. Wasn't I doing it already?

But what about pandemic Chet'la's desires for family? Could I sidewalk chalk before bath and still have time to pursue this life?

Jaila, one of my Saint Paul de Vence travel companions, has known me for as long as Baldwin lived in that town. Our friendship wedded when a cockroach fell just in front of our faces as we headed to the gym our sophomore year of college. We, in true Black girl form, scattered—taking off in different directions. Once we collected ourselves, we cackled. From then on, we were inseparable. We went on long drives to talk, and the conversations morphed from homework and career aspirations to the men we were sleeping with and the women about whom we had fantasies—two budding bi-curious people unable to yet name our queerness. Over the years, our friendship's wattage has varied in intensity, but not the love. When she and her wife asked me to officiate their wedding, I was overjoyed. I say all this to say, we have known each other well and for many years. So, when I stood at the villa window one night, she knew something was wrong.

"I feel heavy," I answered, before I verbal-vomited—charted

the lines I saw between myself and Baldwin. Did my singular focus on my writing cordon me off from another version of my life I also wanted? I didn't see having a family and a writing life as mutually exclusive, but did *I* have enough space for both of them? Especially as a single person? I could do this, come to France for ten days for thoughts and walks, but could I do toddler fevers and prom-date heartbreak? And even if I could, what if it never happened?

In France, I'd already decided I wanted to be a parent and not in the abstract. I was saving for fertility treatments, planning to leave a time-consuming job, moving to a place I had more community support. But still, I continued to try to talk myself out of it. In the same mirror in which I'd hype myself up, I'd also dismantle myself—say it would be too hard on my own, that I should probably remix my relationship to partnership first, that I would be a bad mother, or at the very least, so unlike others that I knew, loved, and admired. In France, those concerns leaked beyond the mirror.

And, with the simplicity and ease that makes Jaila a calming force in our friendship, she reminded me that it's all a choice, that I get to be whoever I want to be, that I have the capacity to change. She reminded me that my motherhood would be as unique to me as hers was to her—her son with his grandmothers, while she and her wife joined me abroad. Two years later, she was the first person I'd call to vent about the low number of Black men who are sperm donors. She and her wife had run into this a few years prior. So when I landed on one, I sent Jaila the profile. She flooded my phone with words of affirmation. Later, she'd flood my phone with condolences and love as I lamented what felt like my body's failures after several unsuccessful fertility treatments, about how I needed to select a new donor. At each turn, Jaila reminded me I wasn't embarking on this alone. I didn't have the two-parent household I was raised in, but I did have community and love. Although I claimed to be afraid of the latter, I often said I had more love in my life than I knew what to do with: Katie cleaning an incision and adjusting a post-op binder; Sara mailing me encouraging notes; Nikki offering her shoulder to soak up my tears; Jaila reminding me to dream my dreams.

On our last day in France, we watched the sunset while having an aperitif in the failing sun's burnt orange. Euros easily fell from my pockets on vinegars, jewelry, and lotions, before going to La Colombe d'Or—one of Baldwin's old haunts—for our last dinner. Amid the dimly lit tables topped with goblets, I took in the fragrant night: the rosebushes, the olive trees, the scent of lemons on the breeze. All of it, the last clasp-click on the suitcase of this trip.

But before that final supper, we wandered up the road where Baldwin's home once sat. It was off a little nook headed out of the ramparted part of town. We pulled up to the relative address and saw the walled-off condos erected where he once lived. Jaila and I hopped out of the car and meandered closer to a gate to see what we could see through its pickets. I saw a structure in the center, which was surrounded by tan ones painted peach by the sun. I told Jaila I thought his actual house was gone, but I wasn't certain.

Just then, a young Black man wandered through one of the gates, carrying building materials. He was one of the first Black people I'd seen outside of our group since arriving in Saint Paul de Vence. Immediately, hoping for a kinship rooted exclusively in pigment, I called after him.

"*Parlez-vous anglais*?" I inquired.

"*Oui*, a little," he responded.

"Do you know if James Baldwin lived here?"

"Who?"

Although we fumbled through a few more sentences, we finally landed on the fact that he didn't know who Baldwin was or if he'd lived there. He was apologetic, and then continued about his business.

Jaila sensed again the gravity, and gave me space to wander alone as she returned to the car. I walked a little farther up the road, taking in the ivy crawling the walls. Saint Paul de Vence was stunning, not a bad place to live and try to write and leave little trace behind. I pulled out my camera and photographed my feet on the road, consecrating this moment, even if only in my digital memory. Baldwin walked here, had for twenty years. And though I had been trying to walk the same path as him, our paths were incomparable, even as we stood on similar ground. I closed my eyes in silent prayer—for him and me and my future baby.

"*Excusez-moi*," I heard. I turned. The Black man jogged toward me. So then, I to him.

He led me back down the road. "Come, come," he said. "He did live here."

As I went to follow him through a metal gate, I hesitated. There was a small group of white faces glaring at me. I stood at the threshold, feeling like a trespasser. The dynamics of it clear: a Black worker, a Black foreigner, and the white people who'd made their home out of the home of a Black writer.

"Can I come in?" I asked, still hesitant.

"If only for a minute or two," one of the white men said, as he waved a flicked wrist in my direction.

"There, over that way," the young Black man said, gesturing to a white building offset from the rest of the modern apartments. I shuffled by and caught a glimmer at the gated gardens, pool, community. I walked around a mature stone pine and snapped a few pictures. When I turned to thank him, he had gone, as had the group of white people.

For a moment, I was alone.

I knew the pergola that overlooked the water wasn't *his* pergola, knew there was no one to ask where his Welcome Table would have been situated, knew that I couldn't walk through the hollows of a house where words left him lonely. Because here, in Le Jardin des Arts, his memory had been extinguished, expelled.

A Moveable Feast

I was raised on the Last Supper—Jesus's final meal with his disciples before he was crucified, before he rose from the dead on Resurrection Sunday. During this meal, where he broke bread and poured wine, he did so knowing he would die. All of his dinner guests shared in this knowledge.

Together, they participated in something sacred.

—

Fellowship as in a group of people with a collective aim.

Fellowship as in a system of shared beliefs.

Fellowship as in a deepening through community.

—

When I was young, my family ate together almost every night. Curry chicken on Mondays. Catfish and salad midweek. And Pizza Fridays. Sundays, the Lord's Day, were for feasting. Each one was like Thanksgiving-lite, with a centerpiece meat and three sides. Actual Turkey Day was more of a food decathlon.

Whether the holiday table was set for three or thirteen, there was a pineapple-dressed ham, a smoked turkey, and a rosemary rib roast braised in its jus for hours. There were garlic mashed potatoes, brown butter broiled into candy for yams, ham hock–bathed collards, and at least two types of stuffing. We held hands, bowed our heads, and thanked God and Son for the fellowship, the nourishment, and the hands, often my mom's, that prepared it.

—

After long days wiping wet counters and crevices of houses and patients, my mother's elders—her mother, her mother's mother, her aunt—shed their uniforms and the small-making ways of the world, the ones that tried to make them a unified blur in the service of white people. At home, they became themselves in floral housedresses—playing rounds of pinochle, hair pinned back to protect fresh presses from the steam of kitchen humidity. They ran their homes with a wood spoon in one hand and commandments in the other, talking shit and telling a kid to go get the milk from the porch. My mother's elders were women who loved not with a kiss or a hug but with a fierce commitment to theirs surviving in this world. The stories of these women—Nana, Aunt Chris, Grandmom Ruth—frothed with food and pots making music: blue crabs and okra, delicately fried calf liver.

Nana was known for her desserts. Although she was a sweet potato pie connoisseur—her crusts the subject of local lore—my father loved her peach cobbler, even though he doesn't like fruit in his pies. Never one for many words but actions—like him—and with a love as vast as her spreads, Nana made my dad a peachless cobbler—just juice and crust—one holiday.

> Food has long been a foundational element to establishing community, especially for Black people. . . . Feeding those we care for is nourishment for the soul.
>
> —EBONY DERR

Nourishment as in sustenance for growth or good health.

My father felt right at home the first time he sat at my Nana's table in 1984—my cousin Tyler's Thanksgiving guest. My late Pop-Pop Raymond joked about how my dad pulled up a chair and went in on a plate (or plural ones) of turkey, collards, and candied yams.

My parents met bent over that food and were married four months later.

Instantly, they were family.

Family as in related by marriage or blood.

Family as in connected by common ancestor.

When I was twenty, I studied abroad in England and spent my first Thanksgiving away from my folks. In a shared dorm kitchen, in Coventry, England, I cooked for hours with Fabienne. Our twenty-year-old fingers traced the lines of recipes from our foremothers as we created our grocery list, as we scoured Tesco shelves for ingredients, as we tasted mashed and stewed bits. My flatmates, from the UK and Russia and Sweden, found our fixings perplexing, their Thanksgiving imaginations paled by whiteness. They were expecting green bean casserole and dressing-stuffed birds, but they didn't know what to say about sweet potato soufflé. As some of it slipped against my palate, I whispered: *home*.

—

Home as in a place in which something originates, a place someone lives.

Home as in family or social unit.

—

At the movies, my brother offered to share his drink with my seven-year-old niece—not wanting to miss the film to get her a refill. She curled her upper lip like she'd smelled rotted fish.

"I don't drink after other people," she asserted.

"But you drink after Mommy?"

"That's different; I'm from her."

In hushed tones in the dark theater, he tried to parse her truth in whisper. The short of it: her father was just some guy her mother married. Not clear on the biology that her parents' shared genetic material led to her, she saw him, in short, as "other people." With the world less muddled by knowledge, where she's from is simple.

Home, for her, similar.

—

Home as in a place in which something flourishes.

In my late teens, I avoided being around the cacophony of my parents' marriage: door slam, splinter of something into shards. I even avoided the tight-lipped silences—a stillness the mere flip of a light switch could break back into noise. Dinners together were no longer a given, none of us wanting to muscle through, so after school, I'd go to Shavana's or Mahsa's. We'd sit down at their kitchen tables: adas polo sprinkled with saffron; herbs and chicken chopped and simmered; homemade roti to sop potato curry from the plate. With their families, we'd swap stories about our days between forks and hands lifted to our faces.

These were the years I overate, celiac making it difficult to be satiated.

Hunger as in a strong desire or craving.

Hunger as in a feeling of discomfort caused by lack or need.

For years, I ate fitfully, nothing that required sitting. Yogurt with plastic spoon. Branch of grapes. Some kind of fruit-nut-grain bar, shoved into my pocket.

I've lived alone since my early twenties, so I've grown accustomed to meals consumed alone and unobserved: pasta from the pot on the stove, loaded baked potato eaten in the bathtub. Mostly, though, these meals consist of me and the TV—the chatter of others prompting me to eat more substantially. But these solo spreads are often punctuated by ones with knees nuzzled close in crowded restaurants or loud laughter in other people's homes as slightly less attended pots boil over.

At the start of the pandemic, I happily set my coffee table for one to the hum of television characters. In April, I started to grow tired of the morning-noon-night monotony of sitting on my couch, counter, bed, consuming calories to *Modern Family*. By May, I started a meal exchange with Andy: his polenta with Bolognese for my chicken tikka masala. Cymone made produce deliveries from her two gardens. I cooked on FaceTime with Diana and Ben: fresh-made pasta for carbonara; gomen, doro wat, and injera. By June, it was warm enough to spread blankets on lawns to enjoy sunshine and salads together.

—

> Domestic spaces . . . house the irreplaceable rituals that take us from one threshold to another.
>
> —SARAH LEWIS

—

Sometimes blankets become kitchen tables.

—

For bell hooks, porches were "places of fellowship," "a democratic meeting place." She saw them as "a revolutionary threshold between home and street . . . [a] liminal space," "a place where the soul can rest."

—

Rest as in intermission of labor, a state of quiet or repose.

Rest as in the cease of movement or work to recover strength, refresh oneself.

Twice a year, I spend ten thirteen-hour days participating in craft lectures, workshops, readings, and meals as a member of the low-residency Master of Fine Arts community at Randolph College. At the top of each of our stretches together, our program director reminds mentors and mentees alike that we won't be able to attend all the things, that we should not try. Engaging for a dozen-plus hours each day isn't sustainable. The schedule accounts for this. There is a three-hour evening break to encourage us to rest and reset. But during each of those pauses, there's an optional faculty meal. And even when my introvert is raw-kneed, pleading for me to *sit it down*, as one of my elders might say, I almost always go to dinner.

Anywhere from eight to eighteen of us congregate at a stream of pushed-together tables for butter chicken and aloo gobi, for burgers and fries, for homemade sausage and sauce and olive tapenade. John will convince Jean to watch *Captain America: Civil War*, while Eloisa laughs that Diana has brought up Andrew Scott again. Chris shares the premise of his script, and Crystal will share some wild hotel shenanigans. Clare and I will both worry about our bags being in each other's way, while Maurice orders cake. Mira will plan our outing to the thrift store, while Lilly and Julia talk about methods for recovering from book tours. Joy will bring up horoscopes, while Anthony pulls up baby photos. I love these makeshift family dinners that remind me of my Nana's Thanksgivings. And when I offer words of love to some of these people at the end of ten days together, as people load their bags into shuttles and cars, I mean them more than when I say it to some with whom I share blood.

—

According to Matthew, at the Last Supper, as Jesus poured wine and broke bread, served it to his disciples, he said, "Verily, I say unto you that one of you shall betray me."

—

> Thou preparest a table before me in the presence of mine enemies: thou anointest my head with oil; my cup runneth over.
>
> —PSALM 23:5
> KING JAMES BIBLE

—

Even the exalted "He" had an enemy at this final feast.

—

> Home is not always the safest place.
>
> —PADMA LAKSHMI

—

Over a kitchen island in Seattle, my great-uncle T mansplained "female empowerment" to the women in my family. My great-uncle Sam hosted brunch—made fresh applesauce and scones, potato latkes and bacon. In retrospect, no one can explain why Uncle T delivered this lecture to his four nieces—a lawyer, an investigator, an education director, and a professor. But at some point in his exegeses, which we let him deliver, he exclaimed how "in the 1950s and '60s, things were really hard for women." That's when we'd decided we'd let him go on long enough, even for an elder. Unclear why the mid-twentieth century was his reference point for when things were "bad for women," we pounced. As voices started to shake the stemware and the family dogs took to their corners, I turned to my eldest cousin and said:

"*This* is why we don't feed wildlife."

Feed as in to fertilize, to add fuel.

My parents had been divorced three years when Nana died in 2023; my dad attended the funeral, sat askance from our family. This was the first time he'd been in the room with people tethered to my mother from birth since the dissolution of their thirty-five-year marriage. I could not tell how he felt being apart from us. I couldn't see beyond myself, nestled into my brother's arms—mourning the woman without whom, because of her generosity and food, I might not be in this room.

At the repast, as plates of green beans and mashed potatoes were scraped, my dad jokingly hopped into the lineage photo with the men in my Nana's line. But maybe it wasn't really a joke; he'd been in the same photo years earlier. When my mother asked him to leave the photo, he laughed and threw his arm around a cousin. She snapped a shot that included him and then asked him to leave again. He didn't. She got upset, said it was another manifestation of his disrespect. He stood sheepishly, then took his leave. Not just of the photo, but of the building.

My Uncle T took this opportunity to say: "He's not family."

Family as in a group bound together by certain shared beliefs or principles.

Family as in a group of connected organisms.

Mahsa and I have shared mealtimes for two decades in Delaware, North Carolina, and New Hampshire; in Maine, Hawaii, and New Zealand. We've grown from lunchtime tacos in the cafeteria and Dairy Queen runs to her blue-veined breast feeding her son and me struggling to fork salad high on post-op Valium. And even though we swim, shop, and travel together, we save tears for food. Aside from funerals, we rarely cry unless we're positioned squarely across from each other at a table.

There, which is often in a packed restaurant, we cannot hide behind HGTV or children's bikes. With our faces in clear view and unobscured by the masks of busyness, we reveal ourselves. Brunch: our meal of choice, bacon salted by our face drippings. We talk about missing our dead (her father; my aunt), about the lives we hope to create, and the chronic conditions that leave our faces in a perpetual state of outbreak. There was the time I cried over breadsticks after getting dumped and the time she sopped up huevos rancheros while worrying about new motherhood. These sessions often conclude with us laughing about crying in public again.

> In most cases, the line between family member and relative is nonexistent.
>
> —THELATHIA "NIKKI" YOUNG

Relative as in connected by common origin, as in dependent on something else.

Relative as in characteristic only in comparison, as in not absolute.

I haven't eaten with my Aunt M since, in my hurt and rage, I told her I wished I didn't have to lose the aunt I loved—implying that that wasn't her.

If I were her, I wouldn't forgive me.

I haven't forgiven my Uncle T.

For me, there are relatives, and there is family. Mahsa is in the latter category.

> The idea of family as a unit oriented toward love, care, choice, and emotional happiness has opened possibilities of diverse unions and even changed the portrait of family makeup in our society.
>
> —THELATHIA "NIKKI" YOUNG

For me, family implies choice and pliability, includes people with whom I break bread regularly.

> Giving people around my table a place where they feel they belong leads to me find my own refuge.
>
> —REEM KASSIS

—

Refuge as in shelter from danger or distress.

Refuge as in . . .
where do I feel safe?

—

> What I write about the land and my place in it is informed by this fact: Sometimes the landscape is of little comfort. Sometimes I want to run far away . . .
>
> —CAMILLE T. DUNGY

—

It has been a long time since I considered myself a Christian, since I believed in a singular, all-seeing God who cares about me, preferring to instead conflate him with "the universe." But I still have an uneven gait from the weight of all the Christian teachings. Psalm 23 imprinted on me like a tattoo I can try to remove but will forever live in my scar tissue.

—

A moveable feast as in a religious meal that doesn't take place on the same calendar day.

A moveable feast as in Passover, Ramadan, Easter.

—

Fifteen years after we cooked Thanksgiving together in Coventry, Fabienne and I eat Indian food together in London. And though over time, our friendship has ebbed and flowed in the tides of adulthood, we fall into a comfortable rhythm as we eat at the bar. Over forkfuls, I ask her what I've been asking myself and others for months: where are you from; where do you call home; where, if anywhere, do you feel like you belong?

Belong as in rightly placed in a specific environment.

At a summer writing retreat, I ate nightly with several people. At these enclaves, where we spend our days in our separate spaces hammering out the words, it is a gift to dine with others who've spent the day doing similar work. I generally look forward to these—an hour or so spent decompressing—but this place made meals quite the production. Usually, I make sure to wipe the crust out of my eyes before heading to a dinner, but at this particular residency, we dressed for the occasion—linen and makeup and jewelry after hours hunched over our desks during a high-humidity heat wave.

The evenings would start in the parlor with Aperol and elderflower spritzes paired with thick-sliced salami and pecorino. We would then roll into glasses of Grillo or sparkling rosé, consumed with mounds of risotto with sprigs of saffron and freshly grated parmigiano in the formal dining room. As the sun started to set behind the villa, dazzling the lake in light, we'd hit our second course of beef filets sprinkled with pink peppercorns, tender chicken topped with butter and sage. And as we poured glasses of Sangiovese and Barolo, we rounded the corner of dessert—fresh apricot tart, tiramisu, scoops of ice cream with fruit. Sometimes we enjoyed this final course on the terrace, if the heat had broken.

What rarely broke, that first week, was the tension. My stomach gnarled as afternoon approached evening. Each night, for the two to three hours we were together, one of the other residents sat at the helm, dominating the conversation. They held court to the backdrop of fleur-de-lis wallpaper, regaling us with conversations of their creative success and sexual prowess. Dinner would drone on, and I'd get quieter—focus on flatware and sconces. After a week of going dead-eyed staring into candlelight, I searched for early flights home. Being curdled over my desk during ninety-five-degree days was hard enough without suffering through a meal with that person every evening. I scoured the faces of my fellow dinner-mates for expressions of exasperation, but each of us, new to one another, kept tight smiles as we nodded at our self-appointed sovereign. But one night, as I looked up across the table, I caught eyes with another Black woman. We held each other's steel-eyed gaze, until I cracked into laughter.

—

> With so much of our Black identity rooted in struggle and ceremony, the moments we can experience true belonging, acceptance, and praise often come when we are among ourselves.
>
> —EBONY DERR

—

Among as in in the company of.

—

In Miami, Kansas City, and Potsdam; in Griante, Ripton, and Jackson; in Flagstaff and Barcelona, Yakima and Madison; in

Lewisburg, Middletown, Keswick, and Richmond, I broke bread again and again with Black women asking some version of the same questions I'd asked Fabienne in London. Sometimes the tables were makeshift, like the low, couch-side ones in a hotel bar in Berlin. Sometimes they were desks in hotel rooms in Mississippi, my friend and I pouring hot water into gluten-free oatmeal pouches. Sometimes the tables were blankets in the middle of another Black woman's yard on a hot pandemic night, as I sobbed and worried I'd never be touched again, as we ate sitting apart from each other.

No matter the table, we talk of miscarriages and leaving jobs; we talk about new love and the wounds of old ones; we talk about the biopsies and hospitalizations, where we can buy headscarves and cowrie-shell bangles. We lament how hard we've pushed to be who we've become and how still we feel we're not enough.

A moveable feast as in a food ritual that can happen any time or place that suits its participants.

In a villa in the south of France, I severed broccoli from their trunks to roast, tossed them in olive oil. I sauteed a wild mushroom medley with thyme and minced garlic, uncorked a bottle of Sancerre to deglaze the mixture in the pan. As the liquid gurgled into its thickness, I seared sage-marinated chicken, before slowly ladling broth over toasted arborio rice. I sat for dinner with my travel companions in our rental's kitchen, windows fogged with condensation, as the fall night cooled off and I launched into my series of inquiries.

Where are you from; where do you call home; where, if anywhere, do you belong?

With a hot forkful pressed to her lips before she blew to cool it, my friend of twenty years answered, "I'm at home. Here. With you. Now."

Home as in fellowship, a place "where the soul can rest."

Home as in a place to be nourished and fed.

Home as in a place that can sometimes be fraught.

But home as in where you go to be with those with whom you belong, with whom you are yourself among.

Epilogue

Turn Here

Who am I to bestow directions for how to find home?

I am still wanderer, blinking blue dot in friends' phones—skittering from front-yard mulch to sandstone gulch, slick dive-bar floor to ivy-hemmed stores.

Each time I creep a coast, I am searching for some semblance of familiar—the girth of the American diner mug, the mute brown of a leopard slug.

But in each new place, I morph my mouth to new turns of phrase, eat French fries with mayonnaise.

Each time asymptoting toward axis, hoping an *elsewhere* will cross paths with a *here*.

Here as in a place where I can laugh without being shushed, wear a caftan and headscarf without second looks.

—

I photograph each place I stay longer than a few days. Shots to document the plots where my roots temporarily took up shop.

This started when I was a teen.

There are photos of townhomes and dorm rooms; the studio apartment on Massachusetts Ave.; the spit of morning on a bedspread; the northern lights' drip from a Philadelphia attic.

Each a quilting square—individual and whole—stitched together into a patchwork.

They bring me closer to and further from my ideas of what could be a *here*.

—

Here, as in *home*.

—

For twelve months, I stayed in no room for longer than a consecutive week or two.

With no permanent address, I clogged my camera with photos of my feet at various thresholds—white Keds, slippers, bare toes.

What a privilege, I thought, to keep arriving somewhere new, to not be connected to *one* place that can become untrue.

—

With mere prefix, a place can be *dis*placed from itself—transformed by forces as fickle as climate change and development.

—

The town of my teen self went from one-laners and four-way stops to two-lane bypasses and roundabouts.

—

So if *home* is not physically identifiable—a state, an address, a zip code—then maybe it's its essence?

—

Plastic-covered wingbacks and a Newport ashed into a Pepsi.

A saw-severed Douglas fir and the reverb of a slapped-down Uno card.

—

> What is home but a cradle of the past
>
> —NATASHA TRETHEWEY

—

My mind swaddles the wobble that follows the closing click of my parents' primary door.

My brother's clean linen and apple-cinnamon scent.

The warmth of my Aunt Gi cuddling me after I finished a third Thanksgiving plate.

The slick varnish on the wood puzzles in the closet next to the basement.

—

> Perhaps home is a memory.
>
> —CAMILLE T. DUNGY

—

But if that's true, then what, with time, will we lose?

—

My brother no longer uses Glade plug-ins.

My father has his own home.

The puzzles are gone, as is my aunt.

—

And what will decay alongside our brain's capacity?

—

Some minds, like boats, know dry docks and steady waters. Others are roiled by storms; perpetually unmoored, they hope to one day find shore.

—

When a glioblastoma chewed through my aunt, she would only list childhood homes on medical forms. The ones from her adulthood excreted.

—

My first clear memory: the dawn of my childhood epilepsy.

I was four in a bright pink nightgown that matched one my teddy bear wore.

A paramedic asked if next time I wanted a helicopter ride.

But if memories are your home, remember that they can haunt. Pink now one of my least favorite colors.

So maybe it's less the recollection and more . . .

> . . . the companions and / or friends who share the memory.
>
> —TONI MORRISON

My brother and I recall my grandmother arriving before the ambulance. No sooner than the phone crested the cradle did she ring the doorbell.

These instances, like photos, an important catalog, an archive of who I've been with and where.

> But I want to have a present-tense relationship with where I'm from.
>
> —SHARA MCCALLUM

—

So maybe instead of the shared memories, *home* is the humans that house them.

—

Niya and me chipping away at a 1,000-piece puzzle for a year, finishing it over wine and good vibes with my mom.

Swimming with Diana and her daughter, with Eloisa and her little one snug inside her endometrium, in the final months of the Mirage hotel's thirty-four-year run.

Mahsa mopping up my post-surgical blood, plunging needles into my gut.

—

They will all root me on through the months I pee on ovulation sticks, through the blood draws and ultrasounds.

They will take me out for oysters and champagne after each failed fertility treatment—the process through which I hope to become a temporary home for you.

—

I hope you can find people who can help warm your bones as you navigate life's tundra.

But just as fire and landscape will change, so, too, will those relationships.

—

Diana's and Eloisa's kids will quickly grow; Niya won't live in the city for long.

And Mahsa wishes she weren't helping me pump my body full of hormones.

I won't call any of them after the third failed treatment when I can't lift myself from the tub, so I cover myself with a towel and cry there, bleeding small rivers for an hour.

Some people who once felt like an arm, may no longer be able to be present without inflicting harm.

In the bone-deep cold of their hurt, an elder I love said my life had no worth.

And I've said similar words to a relative that cannot be unheard.

Even if people are your home, you will still need refuge.

Because there will be times where you'll feel that, too, I have stranded you.

Like a grade school scholar, I'm showing my work—demonstrating what I've done, its lessons, as I cartograph my geography of home in these litanies of words.

—

> [W]riting is a quest of imagination, and the point is to risk the unknown, to become lost without worrying about it, without wondering how I'll get home.
>
> —CARL PHILLIPS

—

Here, in words, I'm less concerned that I'll never get to meet you in this world. In my home of language, I can imagine your laugh splashed against the porcelain of your nightly baths.

—

But if you, like me, find a mainstay in art, you may also find it sometimes leaves you feeling apart.

—

Others may not understand your predilection for diction, why you want to describe the sweet stink of fruit rot or the curt offense of day-old fish innards.

—

> What lengths Elinor would have gone to as a child, what lengths she actually did go to, to feel she belonged to an "us."
>
> —JUNG YUN

—

Make sure not to lose yourself in the quest for words, in your search for a home, a here, or an us.

—

I have been lost.

—

I am a card catalog cabinet—a heavy chest of square-shaped drawers stuffed with slips of paper. Many of those cubes hermetically sealed.

—

When I've been lost, I've been on the run.

From where I'm from.

From people I love.

From—invariably and always—myself.

—

Far away from places I want to be *home*, from the people who, with the slightest tug, could open all my drawers, I hoped to abandon me, become someone I thought worthy of loving.

—

But the farther I run, the more I arrive at myself. My reflection crisp underneath unfamiliar light figures—new moles blossoming on my cheeks in a bathroom in Greece.

In each new place, I arrive at the new nexus of who I might be becoming.

—

I first found my ache for you on a gravel road in the woods of Whidbey Island, on the shores of its Double Bluff Beach, in a sunset over its Useless Bay, as a blue heron, whose stillness stilled me, finally flapped away.

That was 2017.

Since then, you've often visited me: in my dreams on a transatlantic flight to Germany, between the stalls of a Nashville farmer's market, in the haze of a Miami beach nap. You wear a coat my father owned when he was a child.

—

> Perhaps home is not a place but simply an irrevocable condition.
>
> —JAMES BALDWIN

—

I will never be again who I am on this side of being your parent.

—

It's Thanksgiving, and I could be with family or relatives, congregated around warm plates with familiar faces.

Instead, I'm with myself in the quiet of my DC apartment.

—

Earlier I swam in body-temp water, stream pushing down the waist of my suit, before I got the knots beneath my flesh pressed by a massage therapist.

Afterward, I walked toward the memorial of a man responsible for the "founding" of this nation; sat on its steps in front of the Tidal Basin.

From that position, I was at the southmost part of the monuments that make up the National Mall—the base of the foundations of this America.

—

When I returned to my apartment, I called forth my ancestors as I moved pots across a hot stove, slid foil-wrapped pans in the oven: Nana's candied yams, my mother's asparagus.

I invoked my friends: Erica's mac and cheese recipe and Mahsa's Chilean sea bass suggestion.

—

Here with me, amid the stacks of books, flower vessels, and food, are the people who have been bolsters, as I have done all my skittering: messaging me at the lip of the Thames, photographing me dipped in the Caribbean, dancing with me down cracked concrete streets.

—

And now, as the lemon-butter sauce simmers, I listen to the water-woosh of cars and wish I were not cooking for me or them. Instead, I'm longing for you again.

—

Chet'la, be grateful for where you are, I whisper, as I palm my empty abdomen.

—

> Wherever you are is a country.
>
> —MIKKO HARVEY

—

Even when you're in the world gathering elsewheres in your satchel, remember your body is your primary receptacle.

—

> Ground yourself in your body, which is the only home that never leaves you.
>
> —DANTIEL W. MONIZ

—

When I was seventeen, doctors called my mom because they thought they'd misread my bloodwork.

My hemoglobin: 4.8 grams/deciliter.

They took it again; the numbers were the same.

Anything below 6.5 g/dl is life-threatening.

—

After my blood transfusions, my mom laced our fingers: "I'm grateful there's life in these hands."

—

I live in a body that is often in pain—temporomandibular joint dysfunction and pudendal neuralgia, plantar fasciitis and iliotibial band tightness.

I live in a body that is often in a state of confusion—benign rolandic epilepsy, systemic lupus erythematosus, celiac sprue, arrhythmia.

I live in a body that is often unsure of which shore it should moor.

—

Home, for me, has never been simple.

The first four letters of my name is an abbreviation of the city where I was born.

Chet short for *Chester*; *Chet'* short for *Chet'la.*

Chet is rooted in the letter for life; in fortress; in mind, heart, and consciousness.

Chet' has a long memory.

Chet' is both *Chet'* and *Chet*—nicknames used by those whom she finds herself ascribing as *home.*

Chet knows a body can be a home, but it, like place and love, will transform from time or gravity or autoimmune disease.

Chet' wants it to be simpler.

I don't know what *home* is without qualification, complication; I feel similarly about being "American."

I moved to DC in hopes of finding a *here*—drawn to its contradiction, its veil lifted, the mess of what it is to be human.

Our streets boast curated slips of yard and a tire-smashed rat with tail still intact.

Our license plates read "no taxation without representation"—a principle on which the nation was founded—and yet we have no reps in Congress.

But for you, I want *home* to come without the medicinal nip of fresh ginger on a cold-addled throat—without a sting you learn to savor.

If it doesn't, know that I know what it is to wander, to look for a point of origin like Eden or the Big Bang—singularities from which came all existence.

If either of those origin stories is true, it means that I'll always search for what I cannot unearth: the elusive intersection of the Tigris and Euphrates; a place in the night sky that telescopes cannot resolve into image.

If either is ever true, then you are meant to be a wanderer, too.

> Yet if there is no such thing as a true home . . . how is it that we have such a sense for what it is?
>
> —CHRISTIAN WIMAN

One day, you may study Plato's Forms—a metaphysics concept that proclaims there are ideal iterations of everything, but they exist beyond our plane of existence.

We'll only ever experience their spectral remnants.

—

A chair is only ever an afterimage of a Chair—a flash imprinted on our retinas.

—

I'll know how to drink from a glass vessel encased in metal; that a bright-colored gastropod will seep translucent sludge.

But I will never know true Mug or Slug.

—

I've searched for *Home* across sixteen countries and thirty-eight states.

According to Plato, I'll never find it.

—

DC is not *Home*, but it does feel like a lowercase one.

—

Perhaps *home* isn't like Eden or the Big Bang; perhaps it's not a singular person, faith, or place.

—

Perhaps, for me, *home* is in itinerancy; perhaps it's ever evolving.

As long as there is warmth in my hands, maybe *here* and *home* are present-tense and alive—my fingers moored in sandy shore, its soft grit and grip proof that I belong to it.

I wonder what for you will be true.

I don't know. But I hope I can be a *here* and a *home* for you.

Acknowledgments

When I sat in my attic office in June 2020, I never thought the thirty-page chaos document I wrote, trying to process my relationship to this country, would lead me here. Thank you, Kerry Sparks, for believing in those early pages, for helping me mold that myriad of ideas into this book; it wouldn't be the same without you. And thank you to Rebecca Rodd for all of your support.

This book also wouldn't be the same without Maya Millett, who I knew was the editor I wanted to work with upon our first meeting—as we both gathered ourselves one February afternoon on Zoom and quickly broke into an ease that has sustained this editorial journey. Thank you for not only seeing my vision, but supporting its shifts and pushing me to lean further in. I am astounded by how this book has transformed. It's more of me and my poetic self than I imagined possible, as I made this shift to prose; thank you for your constant encouragement. This process has been, even though at times febrile on my end, a dream. And thank you to JP Woodham and everyone else at Dial for your support as we moved through the many stages of this process.

As always, I couldn't have done this without a community of incredible writers and artists who inspired me, who encouraged me, who have reminded me of who I both am and was in this life of letters. Thank you to my early readers: Eloisa Amezcua, Kat Chow, Lana Lin, Martha Park, Joseph Scapellato, Mahreen

Sohail, John Vercher, Jackie Wang, and Shannon Woodloe. I also want to thank Michele Filgate, without whom "Root(les)s: A Genealogy" wouldn't be what it is.

Thank you to my former colleagues at Bucknell University and my current ones at the George Washington University for your support. This book would not have been possible without the funding, time, and support from both of those institutions as well as support from Baldwin for the Arts, the Hawthornden Foundation, and Hedgebrook.

To the Randolph MFA community, you all have impacted this book more than you know through your enduring support. A special thank you to Marie-Helene Bertino for having a cross-legged conversation with me about our shadow selves and Lilly Dancyger for reminding me to say the thing, as we discussed writing about family. And, to Lars Horn, thank you for asking, as I lamented being bored with the essays as I neared my first deadline, if I was bored with them or their structure and shape; these essays wouldn't be the same without your inquiry.

And, finally, thank you to my entire family: from my parents and brother who first taught me how to chase waves to the friends who love and see me in my full humanity. Many of your names appear among these pages as you've housed, fed, and traveled with me along this journey. And though I may have not named each of you here, I am grateful to be in each of your orbits.

Dantiel, Diana, Niya, Nikki, and Sara—I met you all in pursuit of this writing life, but our kinships are so much more than could ever be detailed in these pages. Thank you for holding me infinitely in the light. And Mahsa, there are so few words; I love you THL.

And, finally, Chyrrea and Gordon—thank you for allowing me to tell your stories as I've told my own, for supporting me as I forged into my future. I love you both.

Works Referenced & Consulted

PROLOGUE: TURN WHERE?

Goodwyn, Wade. "Texas Executes Man Convicted in 1998 Murder of James Byrd Jr." *NPR* (April 24, 2019).

Lakshmi, Padma and Jason Wilson. *The Best American Travel Writing 2021* (HarperCollins, 2021).

Marder, Michael. *Philosophy for Passengers* (The MIT Press, 2002).

Morrison, Toni. "The Foreigner's Home," in *The Source of Self-Regard: Selected Essays, Speeches, and Meditations* (Vintage International, 2020).

Thomas, Emily. *The Meaning of Travel* (Oxford University Press, 2020).

PART ONE:

Root(les)s: A Genealogy

Records available through Ancestry.com.

Byng-Hall, John. "The Family Script: A Useful Bridge Between Theory and Practice." *Journal of Family Therapy* 7, no. 3 (1985).

———. *Rewriting Family Scripts: Improvisation and Systems Change* (The Guilford Press, 1995).

Sebree, Gordon. Personal interview. August 2021.

Sebree, Ruth. Personal interview. July 2020.

Todd County, Kentucky (Turner Publishing Company, 1995).

Partus Sequitur Ventrem

Records available through Ancestry.com.

Bates, Niya. Personal interview. January 2024.

Brown, Audrey and Ericka Hill. "2006 African American—Heritage and Ethnography: A Self-Paced Training Resource," Ethnography Program, National Park Service, Washington, DC.

"Corbin Hall," The Virginia Department of Historic Resources.

Corbin Hall Property Owner Association website.

"Edmund/Edmond Scarborough/Scarbrough," A History of the Virginia House of Delegates, Virginia House of Delegates Clerk's Office. https://history.house.virginia.gov/members/725

Hening, William Waller. *The Statues at Large: Being a Collection of All the Laws of Virginia, from the First Session of the Legislature in the Year 1619, Volume V* (W.W. Gray, 1819).

hooks, bell. *Belonging: A Culture of Place* (Routledge, 2009).

Kimmel, Ross M. "Free Blacks," *Blacks Before the Law in Colonial Maryland*, Maryland State Archives, 1974. https://msa.maryland.gov/msa/speccol/sc5300/sc5348/html/chap5.html

"Legacy of Slavery in Maryland," Maryland State Archives. https://msa.maryland.gov/msa/mdslavery/html/research/census1860.html

Long Soldier, Layli. *Whereas* (Graywolf Press, 2017).

Mostafavi, Beata. "Understanding Racial Disparities for Women with Uterine Fibroids," University of Michigan, August 2020. https://www.michiganmedicine.org/health-lab/understanding-racial-disparities-women-uterine-fibroids

Pitts, Jonathan M. "Free Black Men and Women Founded an Eastern Shore Village to Avoid Attention. Now Their Descendants Want to Share the Stories," *Washington Post* (May 24, 2021).

Powers, Kelly. "Free Black People Built an Eastern Shore Village. Why Descendants Want You to Know It's Here," *DelmarvaNow* (March 22, 2022).

Ruane, Michael E. "Experts Probe an Eastern Shore Site, Built by Freed Slaves, for the Nation's Oldest Black Neighborhood," *Washington Post* (July 25, 2013).

Sebree, Chyrrea. Personal interview. August 2022.

Sebree, Chyrrea. Personal interview. October 2024.

Vines, Anissa I., Myduc Ta, Denise A. Esserman. "The Association Between

Self-Reported Major Life Events and the Presence of Uterine Fibroids," *Womens Health Issues* 20, no. 4 (July–August 2010).

Washington, Booker T. *Up from Slavery* (Doubleday, Page and Company, 1901).

"Working Together to Reduce Black Maternal Mortality," Centers for Disease Control. https://www.cdc.gov/womens-health/features/maternal-mortality.html?CDC_AAref_Val=https://www.cdc.gov/healthequity/features/maternal-mortality/index.html

On Homing

Broome, Brian. "I Want to Take the Great American Roadtrip Through the Heartland, But I'm Scared Because I'm, You Know, Black," *The Root* (July 19, 2017).

Elgrably, Jordan. "James Baldwin, The Art of Fiction, No. 78," *The Paris Review* (Issue 91, Spring 1984).

Green, Victor Hugo. *The Negro Motorist Green Book* (Published 1936–1967).

Lincoln, Abraham. "House Divided Speech," National Park Service. https://www.nps.gov/liho/learn/historyculture/housedivided.htm

Lohmann, Kenneth J. and Catherine M. F. Lohmann. "There and Back Again: Natal Homing by Magnetic Navigation in Sea Turtles and Salmon," *Journal of Experimental Biology* (February 6, 2019).

Petrosino, Kiki. *Bright: A Memoir* (Sarabande Books, 2022).

Priest, Joy. "American Honey," *Horsepower* (University of Pittsburgh Press, 2020).

Pruitt-Young, Sharon. "Tens of Thousands of Black Women Vanish Each Year. This Website Tells Their Stories," *NPR* (September 24, 2021).

Resnick, Brian. "Animals Can Navigate by Starlight. Here's How We Know," *VOX* (June 28, 2021).

Sorin, Gretchen. *Driving While Black: African American Travel and the Road to Civil Rights* (Liveright, 2020).

Story of the Year. "Sidewalks," *Page Avenue* (2003).

Mzezewa, Tariro. "2020 Is the Summer of the Road Trip. Unless You're Black," *The New York Times* (June 26, 2020).

Warrant, Eric J. "Unravelling the Enigma of Bird Magnetoreception," *Nature* (June 23, 2021).

Weir, Peter. *Dead Poets Society* (Touchstone Pictures, 1989).

PART TWO:

The Way Forward

Billingsley, Kate T. *A Man of His Time, Playing on Air* Recording (June 21, 2017).

Blakemore, Erin. "Why People Rioted After Martin Luther King Jr.'s Assassination," *History.com* (April 2, 2018).

Boissoneault, Lorraine. "Martin Luther King Jr.'s Assassination Sparked Uprisings in Cities Across America," *Smithsonian Magazine* (April 4, 2018).

Chernick, Karen. "Hank Willis Thomas on *Black Survival Guide* and Creative Civic Action," *Hyperallergic* (August 21, 2020).

Chiasson, Dan. "Claudia Rankine's 'Citizen: An American Lyric'," *The New Yorker* (October 20, 2014).

"The Dred Scott Case," Gateway Arch National Park, Missouri. https://www.nps.gov/jeff/planyourvisit/dredscott.htm

Dungy, Camille T. *Guidebook to Relative Strangers: Journeys into Race, Motherhood, and History* (W.W. Norton & Company, 2017).

Gibbs, Andrea. "1968: MLK Assassination, Riots, and the National Guard Occupation of Wilmington," *WHYY* (April 5, 2018).

Jackson, Lynne. Personal interview. August 2021.

Jones, I.S. *Spells of My Name* (Newfound, 2021).

Judgment in the U.S. Supreme Court Case *Dred Scott* v. *John F. A. Sandford*; 3/6/1857; *Dred Scott, Plaintiff in Error*, v. *John F. A. Sandford*; Appellate Jurisdiction Case Files, 1792–2010; Records of the Supreme Court of the United States, Record Group 267; National Archives Building, Washington, DC.

Levy, Peter B. *The Great Uprising: Race Riots in Urban America during the 1960s* (Cambridge University Press, 2018).

Meier, Allison C. "Drawings of Daily Resistance from the 1956 Montgomery Bus Boycott," *Hyperallergic* (September 3, 2018).

Morretta, Alison. *Slavery and Citizenship: Dred Scott v. Sandford* (Cavendish Square Publishing, 2019).

O'Rourke, Meghan. *The Invisible Kingdom: Reimagining Chronic Illness* (Riverhead, 2022).

Oxford English Dictionary.

Rankine, Claudia. *Citizen* (Graywolf Press, 2014).

Sanfilippo, Pam. Personal interview. August 2021.

Schuessler, Jennifer. "A Fictional Apology to Dred Scott, Born of a Real Family's Painful Legacy," *The New York Times* (May 12, 2016).

Smith, Allan. "The Woman Who Read a Book Right Behind Donald Trump at a Rally Told Us Her Story," *Business Insider* (November 14, 2015).

Walker, Alice. *The Way Forward Is with a Broken Heart* (Ballantine Books, 2001).

Walker, Alice. *Alice Walker: The Official Website.* https://alicewalkersgarden.com/

Winslow, Margaret. "Looking Back to Move Forward: Examining Institutional Racism in Reprising 'Afro-American Images 1971'," American Alliance of Museums (February 11, 2022).

Cases referenced

Winny v. Whitesides (1824)

Scott v. Sandford (1857)

Exhibitions referenced

Black Survival Guide, or How to Live Through a Police Riot

Danny Lyon: Memories of a Southern Civil Rights Movement

The Montgomery Bus Boycott: Drawings by Harvey Dinnerstein and Burton Silverman

Afro-American Images 1971

Afro-American Images 2021

With a special thanks to the National Park Service at Gateway Arch National Park, especially Pam Sanfilippo.

Heart in the Heartland

Badger, Emily and Kevin Quealy. "Where Is America's Heartland? Pick Your Map," *The New York Times* (January 3, 2017).

BouKaram, Fadi. "Lebanon, USA: Meet America's Lebanons. All of Them." https://lebanonusa.com

Brown, Molly McCully. "If You Are Permanently Lost," *Places I Have Taken My Body* (Persea, 2020).

Fountain, John W. "Silent No Longer: Shirley Green Speaks Out, Hoping to Reach Abused Spouses and Their Abusers," *Chicago Tribune* (January 3, 1995).

The Geneva Bible.

"Geographic Center of the Lower 48 United States, Kansas," The Center for Land Use Interpretation. https://clui.org/ludb/site/geographic-center-lower-48-united-states

Green, Al. "Love and Happiness," *I'm Still in Love with You* (1972).

Horn, Cornelia B. "Lebanon in the Holy Scriptures," *The Journal of Maronite Studies* 4, no. 1 (2000).

"How Is the Heartland Region Defined?," Heartland Forward, January 21, 2021.

The King James Bible.

Marsh, Jenni. "Welcome to Lebanon . . . in the United States." *CNN.com* (June 12, 2017).

Online Etymology Dictionary.

Oxford English Dictionary.

Peet, Amanda and Annie Julia Wyman. *The Chair*. Netflix. 2021.

Puccini, Giacomo. *Tosca.* Conducted by Eun Sun Kim, directed by Louisa Muller, performed by Michelle Bradley, Liam Brandfonbrener, Leroy Davis, Rivers Hawkins, Alan Higgs, Anthony Reed, Rodell Rosel, Russell Thomas, and Fabián Veloz. March 18, 2022. Lyric Opera of Chicago.

Schwartz, Stephen. "Thank Goodness," *Wicked: A New Musical*: Original Broadway Cast Recording (2003).

Taylor, Candacy. *Overground Railroad: The Green Book and the Roots of Black Travel in America* (Abrams Press, 2020).

Twain, Mark. *Adventures of Huckleberry Finn* (Penguin Classics, 2014).

Walker, Alice. *In Search of Our Mothers' Gardens: Womanist Prose* (Mariner Books, 2003).

Walker, Margaret. "For My People," *This Is My Century: New and Collected Poems* (University of Georgia Press, 1989).

In the Gallery of Good Hurt

"Art and Artists: The Works of Jabari Jefferson and Titus Kaphar," Thomas Jefferson's Monticello. https://www.monticello.org/exhibits-events/calendar-of-events/ascendant/art-and-artists/

Bates, Niya. Personal interview. March 2025.

Bates, Niya, Chet'la Sebree, and Johanna Heide. "Art and The Archive," *Minor Constellations.* https://minor.hypotheses.org/minor-cosmopolitan-assembly/day-2-nov-11th

Campt, Tina. *A Black Gaze: Artists Changing How We See* (The MIT Press, 2021).

"The Contemplative Site," Thomas Jefferson's Monticello. https://www.monticello.org/visit/tips-for-visiting/contemplative-site

"D.C. Artist Unveils 'Magnolia' Exhibit in Cody Gallery to Highlight Black Women during MLK Week," Marymount University (January 20, 2021).

https://marymount.edu/blog/d-c-artist-unveils-magnolia-exhibit-in-cody-gallery-to-highlight-black-women-during-mlk-week

Durrett, Nekisha. Personal interview. April 2024.

Hannibal, Cecil. "Youngest Freedom Rider Nearly Killed, Imprisoned in Pursuit of Equality," *WAPT 16* (February 11, 2021).

Hyson, Katie. "How Hezekiah Watkins Became the Youngest Freedom Rider—By Accident," *KPBS*, October 18, 2023.

Jefferson, Thomas. *Notes on the State of Virginia* (1787). https://www.monticello.org/thomas-jefferson/thomas-jefferson-and/notes-on-the-state-of-virginia/notes-on-the-state-of-virginia-preface

McGregor, Wayne. *Woolf Works*. The Royal Ballet and Opera (2015).

McGrew, Rebecca. *Alison Saar: Of Aether and Earthe* (Benton Museum of Art at Pomona College, 2020).

Sharpe, Christina. *Alison Saar: Of Aether and Earthe* (Benton Museum of Pomona College, 2020).

Watkins, Hezekiah. *Pushing Forward: The Story of Mississippi's Youngest Freedom Rider* (Dogeared Press, 2019).

Woolf, Virginia. *Mrs. Dalloway* (Harcourt, 2005).

Exhibition labels and descriptions from the following institutions:

Art Gallery New South Wales
Baltimore Museum of Art
Delaware Art Museum
International Slavery Museum
Museum of Contemporary Art Australia
Museum of Modern Art
National Afro-American Museum & Cultural Center
National Civil Rights Museum
National Museum of African American History and Culture
The Phillips Collection
Two Mississippi Museums
Victoria and Albert Museum

Visual art:

Gordon Bennett's *Myth of the Western Man (White Man's Burden)* (1992)

Nekisha Durrett's *James Baldwin* (2019), *Airshaft* (2021), *Magnolia* (2021), and *Frontier* (2023)

Jacob Lawrence's *The Migration Series* (1993)

Jackson Pollock's *Blue Poles* (1952)
Thomas J. Price's *Lay It Down (On the Edge of Beauty)* (2018) and *Signals* (2021)
Alison Saar, *Alchemist*: "the hand is the making of textures"
Alison Saar's *Coup* (2006)

PART THREE:

American Passports

"A Timeline on the U.S.-Led War on Terror," *History Channel*. https://www.history.com/topics/21st-century/war-on-terror-timeline

Billock, Jennifer. "Follow Dante's Footsteps Through Italy," *Smithsonian Magazine* (April 7, 2021).

Brookman-Amissah, Fabienne. Personal interview. March 2023.

"Dante Alighieri," *Poetry Foundation*. https://www.poetryfoundation.org/poets/dante-alighieri

"Dante Alighieri's Tomb," Ravenna Tourism. https://www.turismo.ra.it/en/culture-and-history/memorials/dante-alighieri-tomb

"Iran: Persecution of Bahá'ís," Human Rights Watch (April 1, 2024).

Kfir, Isaac. "Australia's Role in the 'Global War on Terror': Hard Power." *18 Years and Counting: Australian Counterterrorism, Threats and Responses*, Australian Strategic Policy Institute, 2019, pp. 10–11. *JSTOR*, http://www.jstor.org/stable/resrep23062.5

Ohneswere, Shavana. Personal interviews. 2020–2024.

Parvizi, Mahsa. Personal interviews. 2020–2024.

"The Persecution of Bahá'ís in Iran," European Parliament, Parliamentary Question (October 31, 2024).

Purcell, Fiona. "The Faces and Fallout of Australia's Historic Iraq War Protests." *Australia Broadcast Corporation* (May 28, 2024).

Le Jardin des Arts

Als, Hilton. "The Enemy Within," *The New Yorker* (February 9, 1998).

———. *God Made My Face: A Collective Portrait of James Baldwin* (Dancing Foxes Press/Brooklyn Museum, 2024).

Baldwin, James. *Giovanni's Room* (Vintage International, 2013).

———. *Go Tell It on the Mountain* (Vintage International, 2013).

———. *The Fire Next Time* (Vintage International, 1993).

Durie, Alexander. "In Search of James Baldwin's Lost House," *Financial Times* (September 29, 2023).

Farber, Jules B. *James Baldwin: Escape from America, Exile in Provence* (Pelican Publishing, 2016).

Fortin, Jean-Pierre. "White Church or World Community? James Baldwin's Challenging Discipleship," *Journal of Moral Theology* 9, no. 2 (2020).

Glaude Jr., Eddie S. *Begin Again: James Baldwin's America and Its Urgent Lessons for Our Own* (Crown, 2020).

Harris, Jessica B. "Dining with James Baldwin," *Saveur* (May 15, 2017).

"A Place for Gathering, Healing, and Writing," National Museum of African American History and Culture. https://nmaahc.si.edu/explore/stories/place-gathering-healing-and-writing

Zaborowska, Magdalena J. "The Last Days of James Baldwin's House in the South of France: Where Miles Davis, Nina Simone, Stevie Wonder, and More Once Met," *Lit Hub* (April 27, 2018).

A Moveable Feast

Dungy, Camille T. *Guidebook to Relative Strangers: Journeys into Race, Motherhood, and History* (W.W. Norton & Company, 2017).

hooks, bell. *Belonging: A Culture of Place* (Routledge, 2009).

Kassis, Reem. "They Ate at My Table, Then Ignored My People," *The Atlantic* (March 16, 2024).

———. "What Home Cooking Does That Restaurants Can't," *The Atlantic* (May 1, 2023).

The King James Bible.

Lakshmi, Padma and Jason Wilson. *The Best American Travel Writing 2021* (HarperCollins, 2021).

Oxford English Dictionary.

Terry, Bryant. *Black Food: Stories, Art, and Recipes from Across the African Diaspora* (4 Color Books, 2021).

Weems, Carrie Mae, Sarah Lewis, and Adrienne Edwards. *Carrie Mae Weems: Kitchen Table Series* (Damiani/Matsumoto Editions, 2016).

Young, Thelathia "Nikki." *Black Queer Ethics, Family, and Philosophical Imagination* (Palgrave McMillan, 2016).

EPILOGUE: TURN HERE

Baldwin, James. *Giovanni's Room* (Vintage International, 2013).

Dungy, Camille T. *Guidebook to Relative Strangers: Journeys into Race, Motherhood, and History* (W.W. Norton & Company, 2017).

Harvey, Mikko. "Intimacy," in *Let the World Have You* (House of Anansi Press, 2022).

McCallum, Shara. Personal interview. 2023.

Moniz, Dantiel W. Personal interview. 2024.

Morrison, Toni. "The Foreigner's Home," *The Source of Self-Regard: Selected Essays, Speeches, and Meditations* (Vintage International, 2020).

Phillips, Carl. *My Trade Is Mystery: Seven Meditations from a Life in Writing* (Yale University Press, 2022).

Trethewey, Natasha. "Prodigal," *Congregation* (William Meredith Foundation/ Dryad Press, 2014).

Wiman, Christian, ed. *Home: 100 Poems* (Yale University Press, 2021).

Yun, Jung. *O Beautiful: A Novel* (St. Martin's Press, 2021).

ABOUT THE AUTHOR

CHET'LA SEBREE is the author of *Blue Opening*, *Field Study*, winner of the James Laughlin Award from the Academy of American Poets, and *Mistress*, selected by Cathy Park Hong as the winner of the New Issues Poetry Prize and nominated for an NAACP Image Award for Outstanding Literary Work–Poetry. Her essays and poems have been anthologized in Ibram X. Kendi and Keisha N. Blain's *Four Hundred Souls: A Community History of African America, 1619-2019*, Kwame Alexander's *This Is the Honey: An Anthology of Contemporary Black Poets*, and others. Sebree is an assistant professor of English at the George Washington University and teaches at Randolph College's MFA in Creative Writing program.

https://www.chetlasebree.com
IG: @cnsebree
X: @Nahtil

Books Driven by the Heart

Sign up for our newsletter
and find more you'll love:

thedialpress.com

@THEDIALPRESS

@THEDIALPRESS

Penguin Random House collects and processes your personal information. See our Notice at Collection and Privacy Policy at prh.com/notice.